SURVIVAL STRATEGIES
FOR AFRICANS
IN AMERICA

Books by Anthony T. Browder

From The Browder File:
22 Essays on the African American Experience

Exploding The Myths Vol. I:
Nile Valley Contributions to Civilization

From The Browder File Vol. II
Survival Strategies for Africans in America

Egypt on the Potomac
A Guide to Decoding Egyptian Architecture and Symbolism in Washington, DC

Avatar Revisited
A Historical and Cultural Analysis

Finding Karakhamun
The Collaborative Rediscovery of a Lost Tomb

With Atlantis T. Browder

My First To Africa

Africa On My Mind
Reflections on my Second Trip

FROM THE BROWDER FILE VOL. II

SURVIVAL STRATEGIES
FOR AFRICANS IN AMERICA
13 Steps To Freedom

by
Anthony T. Browder

The Institute of Karmic Guidance
Washington, D.C.

FROM THE BROWDER FILE VOL. II

SURVIVAL STRATEGIES
FOR AFRICANS IN AMERICA
13 Steps To Freedom

by Anthony T. Browder

Published by
The Institute of Karmic Guidance
P.O. Box 73025
Washington, DC 20056
301-853-2465 voice
301-853-6027 fax
www.ikg-info.com

Cover Illustration: Paradigm Enterprises

Publication Layout & Design: Tony Browder

Library of Congress Catalog Card Number: 89-80061

ISBN# 978-0924944-10-9

14th Printing / April 2020
Printed in Canada

Paperback $20

Dedication

This work is dedicated in loving memory of
my grandmother, Mary Elizabeth Walker, and
my dear friends Listervelt Middleton and Marie Hollis.

Acknowledgments

This work exists because of the encouragement and support I've received from those who have read and loved the first volume of *From The Browder File*. Acknowledgments must also be given to those who have read this manuscript, in its various forms, and have helped me fine tune and focus my thoughts. They are: Michelle Padgett, Greg Thomas, Krystal Thurmond, Janice George, Paul Coates, Karin Norington, Paul Lane and Reginald Scott. Thanks to G. Kemet Uhuru for the cover art, Rufus Wells for the cover layout, Mosi Chamberlain, William Maxwell, and Clyde McElvene for photography and text layout; and Ruby Essien and Anne Browder for their editorial expertise.

Special thanks to Kwabena Brown for showing me the path, and Atlantis Browder for making fatherhood a true joy.

About the Cover

The cover art was inspired by the painting "The Mask" by renowned African American artist, Carl Owens. Owens' work was inspired by an ivory mask which was carved by an unknown African artist in the 16th century. In 1992, Paradigm Enterprises created the design, "Man of Africa," which now graces the cover of *Survival Strategies*. Paradigm's design has been reproduced on clothing and other products and is one of my favorite works of art. It wonderfully represents the spirit of *Survival Strategies* and was reproduced courtesy of G. Kemet Uhuru. The cover art is significant for several reasons. The face is a vivid reminder of our African origins, and the chains represent the hardships that Africans on the continent, and Africans in America, have endured over the last 500 years. The Medu Netcher, (hieroglyphics), in the background, symbolizes the legacy of Africans in the Nile Valley which has inspired the African Centered movement and helps us break the chains of mental slavery.

Cover Art By
Paradigm Enterprises
P.O. Box 349
Morristown, NJ 08057-0349
(609) 321-0650

Cover Art Colorized By
Rufus Wells
(301) 963-2507

Cover Design By
Tony Browder

Table of Contents

Part Three: SPIRIT

Preface

Many people are capable of looking back on their lives and identifying events that profoundly affected the way they saw themselves and their place in the world. I experienced such an event in the winter of 1980 during my first study tour of Egypt. Throughout my trip, I became increasingly aware that I had been mis-educated throughout my years of formal schooling. During my tour of Egypt, I saw numerous examples of a glorious ancient African legacy that had been distorted and falsely attributed to persons of a lighter hue and of foreign origins. For the first time in my life, I was beginning to see the world through "African eyes." I was thrilled and overwhelmed by the possibilities this new outlook presented.

On my return to the United States, I was consumed by an intense desire to share my experiences with my family, friends, and anyone who was willing to listen. During the following year, my desire to share my experience with a broader audience became a reality when I was offered an opportunity to conduct a seven-week lecture series on Ancient Egyptian history at the University of Maryland. The series was well received, and later that year, I offered it at several locations in the District of Columbia.

The public response to the lectures exceeded my expectations and prompted me to rededicate my life to documenting the "positive portrayal of the worldwide African experience." I sought information that validated the glory of Ancient Africa and confirmed the presence of a spiritual force that still influences Africans throughout the world. My research has centered on the areas of Ancient Egyptian history, culture, philosophy, symbolism, architecture and spirituality—and their combined influence on Western civilization.

I have been in the information business since 1982 when I founded the Institute of Karmic Guidance as a vehicle to disseminate my research. The significance of my work was impressed on me at another eventful gathering during Black History Month in 1990 when I was invited to give a keynote address at a government agency in Washington, D.C. On my arrival at the facility, I was informed by the sponsors of the program that they were a division of the Central Intelligence Agency (CIA). As I was introduced to the audience by the director of the facility, I was shocked to hear him declare that I was in the same business as their organization except that I gathered information "relative to the survival of Black people." That was a flattering comparison, but it also caused me to re-evaluate the scope of my work and its impact on the lives of people who have been mentally and spirituality robbed through mis-education.

I have recently come to understand the significant role agencies that gather intelligence data play in analyzing and disseminating information. The quality of the information gathered is crucial to the success of any intelligence operation. Accurate details must be collected, analyzed, and distributed to individuals "with the need to know," who will then implement the appropriate strategies to insure the continual empowerment of the organization, group, or nation.

Intelligence gathering is a painstakingly serious occupation that involves many sacrifices and risks. However, the benefits gained from the analysis and application of new data are well worth the challenge. It could mean the difference between annihilation, marginal survival or living a life of limitless potential for current and future generations. I was intrigued by the idea and possibilities of using intelligence/information to liberate the minds of African people.

Prior to this speaking engagement, I considered myself just another "Black History Month" presenter. However, I have since developed a greater appreciation for my work and a deeper commitment to share my research with the African American community. This "intelligence," when properly analyzed and implemented, can empower us and assure our survival in a society that is growing increasingly complex and hostile.

I have also come to understand that the hostility we exhibit toward each other stems from years of mis-education and unresolved personal conflicts. Because of our limited access to, and appreciation of African history and culture, we currently function at varying levels of awareness and personal development. We Africans in America have been socially engineered to reject our past, and far too many of us live in a state of suspended animation. We deny the historical realities confronting us daily. Too many of us mistakenly believe that the past has no bearing on the present and is unrelated to the future. Thus, we have been conditioned to live our lives disconnected from cultural values, principles, and ideals essential for peaceful living. This publication is designed for persons who earnestly desire knowledge that will lead to a change in consciousness. It is hoped that the contents of this publication will be embraced in the true spirit of *Harambee* and *Sankofa*. This book proposes to teach Africans in America how to pull together collectively and reclaim our past in order to build a meaningful future for ourselves and our descendants.

Survival Strategies For Africans in America was written specifically to help "recovering Negroes," and former "black people" become "Born Again Africans." It is meant to inform and not to offend. It consists of useful information that, when dutifully applied, will allow us to break free of the invisible bonds of oppression designed to stymie our mental, physical, and spiritual development and to prevent us from becoming self-determining people.

Self-determination is a natural by-product of self-awareness, and together they form the mental and spiritual cornerstones of freedom. *Survival Strategies For Africans in America* comprises 13 Steps, that lead us from self-awareness to self-determination. Steps 1 through 5 relate to the African Mind; Steps 6 through 9 reference the African Body; and Steps 10 through 13 discuss aspects of the African Soul. The methodology allows for the complete integration of the 13 Steps so that the newly developed consciousness will lead to Freedom. By following these steps we will ultimately enter into the realm of self-empowerment and personal well-being.

The material in this publication has been carefully researched and is now presented to the African family for review and consideration. It is hoped that these *Survival Strategies* will inspire us to continually seek truth in all of our endeavors and to achieve and sustain the freedom that is long overdue.

Introduction

How to use This Book

In 1987, I began writing a bi-weekly newspaper column from which I later selected twenty-two articles for a collection of essays that was published in 1989 as *From The Browder File: 22 Essays on the African American Experience*. In the time that has passed since those articles were written, my faith has been tested, my understanding has deepened, and my commitment to the African spirit within me is stronger now than ever before.

Enthusiastic responses from thousands of people who have read *From The Browder File* prompted me to write this second volume of essays. I have often been told of the liberating effect that *The Browder File* has had on the lives of those who have read it, and I am frequently asked by my readers, "What should I do now, how do I use this information?"

Survival Strategies for Africans in America: 13 Steps to Freedom, was written in direct response to those questions. I have broadened the scope of much of the material presented in the first volume of essays and provided additional insights that will lead to the stated goal: Freedom.

This book, however, was not written exclusively for African Americans. With minor modifications, these Steps may be used by Africans living in any corner of the world. I have found that no matter where on the globe African people live, we are all subjected to the same oppressive forces of racism and white supremacy. Fortunately, we also have access to the same liberating Spirit of the Creator.

The 13 Steps to Freedom contain three categories that relate to the liberation of the African Mind, Body, and Spirit. Each step is an individual lesson that should be studied and applied before proceeding to the next step. Each Step is divided into three components to help facilitate your understanding.

The first component represents the *Voice of Inspiration*, which frequently speaks to us and silently plants liberating ideals in our minds. When these ideals are properly nourished, they spring forth from our consciousness as vibrant thoughts that move us into action. This component is presented in *italicized* type and precedes the title of each Step. The only exception to this format is in Steps 6 through 9, which are covered by one component.

The second component is the thoughtful realization of Inspired Ideals. It provides an in-depth analysis of the issue and evaluates its personal, and cultural significance.

The third component offers a practical approach for incorporating the pertinent aspects of the thoughtful realization into your daily life. This segment is a prescription for mental, physical and spiritual well-being and is preceded by the ancient African symbol ☜, which is called the *Uchat Eye*.

When all 13 Steps are mastered and linked, they form a practical and symbolic stairway to Freedom. On a practical level, freedom is defined as the "exemption or liberation from the control of some person or arbitrary power." Symbolically, freedom also means the *free*, or unrestricted use, of the *dome*--the head or mind.

Freedom of the mind is our primary objective because once it is achieved it makes other goals readily identifiable and, therefore, easily attainable. The mind is the conduit through which a person can access spiritual consciousness. If the mind is constrained and filled with thoughts of negativity and inferiority, it is incapable of tuning in spiritually empowering thoughts. A self-constrained mind is programmed to engage in self-destructive behavior that is often injurious to the body. To paraphrase a frequently used statement in the African American community, "If you free your mind, your behind will follow."

For thousands of years, it has been known that the mind is a conduit that attracts ideas and energies from the universal elements that duplicate and enhance the thought process. To that extent, you are what you think, and your potential for future development has already been determined by those who have programmed your mind.

xvii

For those of you who are ready—now is the time to wrest control of your mind from those who would keep you mentally and spiritually enslaved. Now is the time to take the first of many steps that will allow you to grow beyond the constraints that have kept you functioning in "survival mode." Freedom can be achieved if you are willing to take conscious and deliberate steps in its direction. If you are ready, let the journey begin.

Survival Strategies For Africans In America
13 Steps To Freedom

M I N D

STEP 1. Racism and White Supremacy Are the Most Persistent Problems Confronting Africans in America

STEP 2. Become Aware of the Power of the Media

STEP 3. Perception Precedes Being . . . You Are Who You Believe You Are

STEP 4. Information Is Power, But Power Is Nothing Without Control

STEP 5. Empower Your Mind . . . See the World Through African Eyes

B O D Y

STEP 6. Become Aware of the Uniqueness of Your African Body

STEP 7. Develop Cultural and Holistic Approaches to Health

STEP 8. Become Aware of Your Mind/Body Relationships

STEP 9. Familiarize Yourself with the Mysteries of Melanin

S P I R I T

STEP 10. Learn to Interpret Religious Imagery

STEP 11. Learn to Honor the Memory of Your Ancestors

STEP 12. Learn to Prepare Yourself for War and Peace

STEP 13. Learn How to Live in the New America

Part One

MIND

The United States of America was conceived in sin. Liberty and Justice are "Uncle Sam's" adopted parents and their names were duly recorded on his birth certificate on the 4th of July in 1776. The identity of this nation's true parents has been a well guarded secret for over two centuries. The mere mention of their names evokes a chorus of denials from his offspring—the echoes of which can be heard reverberating from "sea to shining sea." Despite numerous detractions, America's family records have been carefully searched. Blood tests have been conducted, and the genetic evidence has been carefully analyzed, which confirms, beyond a shadow of a doubt, that racism and white supremacy are the true parents of this nation.

Knowledge of America's true parentage is of grave importance, particularly if America's stepchildren, Africans in America, wish to live truly meaningful lives. The European Americans' declarations of independence were a hollow mockery rife with contradictions to the enslaved Africans and the indigenous population of this land. What kind of mind would create a nation where all men were deemed equal in the eyes of God except red men and black men?

If you study the development of early Europeans, you will begin to see how they have historically viewed the world and its inhabitants. By examining the history of racism and white supremacy, you will also gain a deeper understanding of the numerous challenges that confront you in America.

STEP 1.

Racism and White Supremacy
Are the Most Persistent Problems Confronting
Africans in America

Racism and white supremacy were the motivating ideologies behind the British Colonist's drive to exterminate Native Americans and assume control of their land. Racism and white supremacy were also responsible for creating and sustaining the conditions which led to the enslavement, death, and disenfranchisement of millions of Africans and their American descendants.

Throughout the last four and a half centuries, racism and white supremacy have continually threatened the existence of African people before, during, and after their enslavement. These threats have forced Africans to modify their beliefs, thoughts, and behavior in order to survive on a planet where they are regarded as "Third World" people. Those who now claim to be members of the "First World" are actually late comers to the human family.

Africans were the first human beings on earth. They gave the world its earliest culture, civilization, and conceptualization of God. Mankind continues to benefit from the African interpretation of universal forces that affect every living thing. Africans in America will never know these truths as long as they continue to view the world through the eyes of their former slave masters.

In order for Africans to understand the nature of the world in which they live, they must first understand the nature of the people who interpreted the world for them. This interpretation determined their perceptions of reality and dictated how they now function in the world. Since the world of the contemporary African has been shaped by racist ideologies formulated long ago, it is necessary to understand the roots of racism and white supremacy in order to correctly interpret current events and formulate meaningful plans for the future.

Contrary to popular belief, there is no such thing as race. Race is a false construct which was created by Europeans, hundreds of years ago, in order to differentiate themselves from people of African descent and other people of color throughout the world. The concept of race was created by scientists and scholars at Gottingen University in Germany between 1775 and 1800. During this twenty-five year period, these "scholars" invented the word *Caucasian*, divided humanity into races, and contended that the white race was superior.

The illusionary myth of race has been in existence for only two centuries but it pales in comparison with the ideology of white supremacy and the system of racism that it spawned. The power inherent in the concept of *white supremacy*, along with the mere utterance of those words, create within the mind, semantic and visual perceptions of "black inferiority." If one believes that white is superior, then anything that is non-white, colored or black is perceived as inferior. If white is holy and pure, then black must be ungodly and evil. As crazy as it seems, this convoluted logic has been used by "civilized men" (scholars, scientists, theologians, politicians, and others) for hundreds of years to justify the murder and enslavement of people of color.

If Africans are to survive in America, they must confront the inescapable realities of racism and white supremacy. They must be aware that their ancestors have battled these oppressive foes for over fifteen generations and that freedom will not be achieved by prayers and dreams alone.

The liberation of the African Mind, Body, and Spirit can only be achieved through the use of an African centered value system that makes the study of the successes and failures of the past the highest priority. Many ethnic groups have struggled to survive in America, and those who have achieved a meaningful measure of freedom, have wisely maintained their ancestral roots. Clearly, the road to the future begins in the past.

The prevailing belief among paleontologists, geneticists, and anthropologists is that humanity began in Africa over 200,000 years ago. Scientific evidence suggests that the first humans left their birth land, and after thousands of years populated the rest of the world. By virtue of their birthplace, the first humans responsible for populating the planet were not "Negroes;" they were Africans.

What this evidence suggests is that the first people who inhabited the lands that we now call *Europe* looked nothing like the people who live there today. As one would imagine, there are varying opinions as to how Africans became Europeans. In order to understand how this transition occurred, we must rely on scientists from a variety of disciplines to reconstruct the ancient beginnings of mankind. With the advent of recent breakthroughs in genetic testing and new archeological discoveries, we are beginning to get a clearer picture of the past events that shaped our current reality. We now know that the Earth has undergone upheavals that profoundly influenced the development of humanity. It is generally believed that the last ice age, which occurred between 75-12,000 years ago, created environmental conditions that led to the transformation of dark-skin people to light-skin people. There are many texts that discuss these events but, Dr. Charles Finch, a physician and researcher, has provided an in–depth analysis of "Race and Human Origins" in his book *Echoes of the Old Darkland*. Finch provides a concise discussion of various theories and complex issues pertaining to human development. He offers the following conclusions:

- For seven million years, the hominid line leading to modern man emerged, evolved, and attained its final form in eastern Africa.

- Modern man, *Homo Sapien Sapien*, evolved entirely in Africa about 200,000 years ago.

- The emergence of ethnic variations of the original African type, took place between 50-30,000 years ago.

- Modern man came to occupy Asia at least 75,000 years ago.

- Modern man came to occupy Western Asia (Europe) between 50-40,000 years ago.

- The earliest "European Caucasian" evolved from the African between 30-25,000 years ago in an Ice-Age environment near the southern limit of the great line of European glaciers along the 51st parallel of southwestern Russia.

When the aforementioned data are compiled and analyzed sequentially, they present a convincing story of the conditions which led to the evolution of the modern European.

Nearly 75,000 years ago, the "Northern Cradle" of Western Asia (now called Europe) was covered by glaciers about one-mile thick on average. These glaciers extended from the Arctic circle, "across southern England, northern Germany, Poland, and southern Russia," forming a barrier that prevented people from entering or leaving the affected areas.   For over 60,000 years, these icy conditions existed and the human beings trapped behind the wall of ice were forced to adapt to their new surroundings or perish. Those who survived did so by hunting wild animals for food, draping their bodies with the fur of their prey, and finding warmth and shelter in underground caves.

The harsh weather conditions in Western Asia subjected the cave dwellers to numerous hardships, and also played a role in transforming their physical appearance.   The diminished amount of sunlight in the northern hemisphere, coupled with frequently overcast skies, caused the skin of the cave dwellers to gradually become lighter.

Scientists now understand that this was caused by genetic mutation, which occurred because of a shrinking gene pool, and the adaptability of the human body to new environmental conditions. In the extreme North of Western Asia (Europe), black skin became "an adaptive liability" for two reasons: 1) it was more susceptible to frostbite, and 2) it limited the absorption of adequate amounts of Vitamin D, which is essential for healthy bone formation.

Medical studies of soldiers who fought in Korea and both World Wars showed that African American troops were five times more likely to develop frostbite than their European or European American counterparts.   Such data led physicians to conclude that white skin is more cold-resistant than black skin.   Dr. Finch, citing research from the *Journal of Physiology*, states that, "There is also a three-to-five times greater penetrance of ultraviolet light in white skin compared to that in black skin."

Medical research has also shown that Africans living in the northern latitudes have a susceptibility to rickets that is 2-3 percent higher than that of Europeans.   Rickets is a disease of the skeletal system that causes the bones to weaken and is often the result of a Vitamin D deficiency.   Rickets is also caused by an absence of sunlight.   Under ideal conditions, the melanin in the skin of Africans filters out the harmful (ultraviolet) rays of sunlight that can cause skin cancer but allows in enough ultraviolet light for the skin to produce Vitamin D.   In a colder environment, where there is less sunlight, melaniated skin is always a liability, thus, in order for "black skinned" humans to survive during the Ice Age of Northern Europe, they had to mutate and develop "white skin." It is a generally accepted view that the transformation from "black skin" to "white skin" people occurred over a period of 10-20,000 years. What is now coming to light is that this transformation not only affected the color of skin and eyes, the texture and color of the hair, but also produced changes within the brain that influenced human consciousness. Scientists and researchers now know that the absence of sunlight alters the function of the pineal gland and inhibits its ability to produce sufficient amounts of two essential hormones--melatonin and serotonin.

The pineal gland is a small organ in the middle of the brain. Throughout the early twentieth century, medical schools taught their students that it was a "vestigial sensory organ" that served no known purpose. This belief was based upon the study of Europeans whose pineal gland was found to be calcified in 85 percent of the population. When pineal research was broadened to include people of African ancestry, it was discovered that they had a pineal calcification rate of only 15 percent.

Within the last twenty years, the medical community has revised its opinion of the pineal gland. While its function is not fully understood, it is regarded by many as the "master gland" in the body because the hormones it secretes are essential for "normal" human development.

It is interesting to note that during the 1980s, public discussions of melanin, melatonin, and the pineal gland were often limited to a handful of African American scholars who held annual Melanin Conferences. Their research was often regarded as "pseudoscientific," and ignored by mainstream (European) scientists for over a decade. However, in 1995 there was an explosion of interest in melatonin, and dozens of European scientists began touting it as the wonder drug of the ages. Throughout 1995, various publications, and television and radio programs, informed the public of melatonin's ability to retard the aging process, regulate sleeping patterns, improve sex performance, and improve health, vitality, and longevity.

Because of media attention, the public's interest in melatonin and the function of the pineal gland increased substantially. While medical science has yet to fully understand the various functions of melatonin in the body, it has acknowledged that insufficient amounts of melatonin causes the body and mind to degenerate at an accelerated rate and thus inhibits its performance. I have been aware of the significance of melatonin for over fifteen years. It is interesting to note that melatonin became a household word only after it had been synthesized, commercialized, and marketed for mass consumption by those who are unable to produce it naturally. Issues pertaining to melanin, melatonin, hormones and the pineal gland will be discussed in greater detail in Step 9.

There are numerous African American scholars whose research on melanin has come to my attention over the years. Richard King, M.D., one of the leading melanin researchers in the African American scientific community, frequently refers to melatonin as a "civilizing hormone." Dr. King is a psychiatrist and author. His research has led him to conclude that insufficient amounts of melatonin in the body often result in abnormally aggressive patterns of behavior.

Frances Cress Welsing, M.D., is another prominent African American psychiatrist and researcher. She is best known for her study, *The Cress Theory of Color Confrontation and Racism (White Supremacy)*, which revolutionized people's perceptions of race and racism. Dr. Welsing theorized that the current system of racism is a manifestation of the European's fear of genetic annihilation. This fear grew out of the Europeans' realization that genetically they are a recessive minority in a world that is predominately inhabited by melaniated people. This fear led to the development of a collective "genetic inferiority-complex" that later manifested itself in the establishment of a global system of white supremacy.

Thus, the diminished presence of melanin and melatonin in Europeans, coupled with the realization that "they" were a minority in a world predominately inhabited by people of color, were critical factors in the development of the false belief in the superiority of "white skinned" people. This belief escalated considerably after 1492 and has served as the catalyst for the development of the current system of European global domination. During the fifteenth and sixteenth centuries, as European explorers traveled throughout the world, they "discovered" lands inhabited by people of color—humans with black, brown, red, and yellow skin. Whenever they had intercourse with women of color, their offspring were always "colored." Thus, the fear of being alone in a world of color, coupled with the inability to reproduce their own kind from "interracial" mating, established deep seated fears within the European mind. The only way they could rule the world was by implementing a global program of deception, destruction, and domination. The nature of the society which we have inherited, was forged in a crucible of fear and ignorance. It was established centuries ago and perpetuated worldwide. Dr. Kwame Nantambu, associate professor of Afrocentric Geopolitics at Kent State University, has written numerous publications that examine the relationship between racism, white supremacy, economics, and global politics. In his latest book, *Egypt and Afrocentric Geopolitics*, Dr. Nantambu provides an historical analysis of how Europeans achieved global domination.

> In 1492, Europeans controlled only nine per cent of the world; within three hundred years afterwards, they colonized one–third of global humanity. By 1880, Europeans ruled over two–thirds of the globe. By 1935, they were in political control of not only eighty–five per cent of the planet's resources but also seventy per cent of the world's population; in the 1990's, Europeans now control eighty–five per cent of the world's population through its weapon of geopolitics or the 'new world order.'

Race, racism and white supremacy are ideologies which are the by-product of a xenophobic consciousness that has been imposed upon the majority of the inhabitants of the planet. Terms such as the *white man's burden* and *manifest destiny* express the Europeans' belief in their God-given right to conquer the world and introduce "civilization" to people of color. According to this doctrine, the whiter your skin, the greater your intelligence and the more privileges you are entitled to. To this end, racism and white supremacy are the power behind the most destructive forces the world has ever witnessed. Racism and white supremacy are synonymous and must never be confused with acts of prejudice—they are as different as night and day.

All people have prejudices; this may be considered to be one of humankind's great failings. However, for a group to be legitimately classified as *racist*, it must possess the power to impose its prejudices on members of other ethnic groups. Power transforms a "pre-judged belief" into an ideology that is popularized, legitimized, and finally, incorporated into the legislative, judicial, religious, and social system designed to control the powerless. The system of racism/white supremacy was created to sustain the white minority global dominance over the colored majority populations. Racism/white supremacy insures its control by influencing the thought and behavior of those who benefit from the perpetuation of this ideology, as well as its intended victims. Dr. Welsing has researched this subject extensively and has identified "nine areas of people activity" that are controlled by racists and white supremacists that exert wide ranging influence on society. The nine areas include: *economics, education, entertainment, labor, law, politics, religion, sex, and war.*

By understanding the origins and development of humanity, the evolution of mankind, and the conditions which led to the creation of the *European*, Africans can begin to see the world from a truly different perspective. By looking at world events from this point of view, there can be no doubt that the presence of Africans in the Americas and the current conditions of Africans in Africa are the direct result of survival strategies implemented by racist white supremacists over five hundred years ago. The events of the past do not dissipate; they set into motion a chain of events that transcend time and space and shape the present.

Consider this brief timeline of European and African relations as links in a chain that was forged in Europe and currently binds Africans in America:

- In 1441, twelve kidnapped Africans were presented as a gift to Prince Henry of Portugal.

- In 1442, Pope Eugenius IV granted Europeans permission to enslave Africans whom he regarded as soulless individuals.

- In 1444, Europeans began "importing" Africans into Europe and enslaved them in the Americas less than a century later. These actions, over the next 400 hundred years, resulted in the death and enslavement of over 100 million people of African descent.

- In 1665, the colony of Maryland enacted legislation declaring that "black people shall constitute an available, uncompensated . . . permanently subordinated work force, which shall be separated from the white society."

- In 1857, the Supreme Court's Dred Scott decision, declared that African Americans were not citizens of the United States.

- In 1885, after 450 years of enslaving Africans, fourteen European nations met in Berlin to decide how they would divide Africa among themselves and colonize its inhabitants.

- In 1896, nineteen years after African Americans were granted citizenship, the United States Supreme Court in Plessy v. Ferguson formally established the doctrine of "separate but equal" to justify the continuation of racial segregation.

- In 1964, Congress passed a Civil Rights Bill officially banning discrimination in housing, education, and employment. However, the Civil Rights Bill of 1990 was vetoed by President Bush because he feared it would "introduce the destructive force of quotas."

- In 1992, the Supreme Court set limits to the 1965 Voting Rights Act and struck down a "hate crime" law that banned cross burnings.

- In 1995, the United States Congress passed legislation insuring that African Americans would receive prison sentences for drug possession of crack cocaine at a ratio of 500 to 1 compared with possession of powder cocaine used by European Americans.

- In 1996, an investigative reporter for the *San Jose Mercury News* alleged that the CIA played a major role in the introduction of powder and crack cocaine into the African American community in an effort to finance anti-Communist forces in Nicaragua during the 1970s and 1980s.

Singularly, these events may be seen by some as isolated events that have no bearing on the present and do not constitute a specific pattern of behavior. However, when considered from an enlightened and well-informed perspective, it can be shown that the historical relationship between Africans and Europeans has been filled with strife and turmoil that will likely continue until power is more equally shared.

If racism and white supremacy were not a persistent problem in America, Africans would not have been enslaved, there would have been no Civil War, there would be no need for affirmative action programs, nor would there now be a debate concerning the merits of continuing such programs. The presence of a racist and white

supremacist consciousness in America led to the enactment of
constitutional amendments, the establishment of numerous civil
rights organizations, such as the NAACP (National Association for
the Advancement of Colored People), SNCC (Student Nonviolent
Coordinating Committee), SCLC (Southern Christian Leadership
Conference), CORE (Congress Of Racial Equality), and the
development of HBCU's (Historically Black Colleges and
Universities.)

Over the centuries, African Americans were told by their
oppressors to "lift themselves up by their bootstraps." Even though
many African Americans were "bootless," some who attempted to
uplift themselves found the boot of their oppressors weighing
heavily on their backs. Other Africans overcame oppressive forces
but never fully enjoyed the fruits of their labor because of the
enactment of local, state, and federal legislation that prevented
the accumulation of wealth and power.

Numerous laws, also called "Black Codes," were written to
ensure that skilled African Americans could not secure licenses,
open businesses, and compete fairly with European American
businessmen. Many of these Black Codes were written when chattel
slavery ended and they remained in effect for almost one hundred
years.

Despite these obstacles, U.S. history is replete with numerous
examples of African American men and women who overcame
tremendous odds to establish businesses, buy land, and develop
their communities. Typically, whenever African American
professionals were prohibited from joining European American
business or professional associations, they formed their own. For
example, the African American physicians prohibited from joining
the American Medical Association established the National
Medical Association in 1895. The same is true of the African
Americans who formed the National Dental Association in 1913
and the National Bar Association in 1925.

The ever-prevailing presence of racism/white supremacy in
America has continually forced African Americans to fend for
themselves, sometimes with disastrous results. In the early 1900s,
the African American business district in Tulsa, Oklahoma was
deemed the most prosperous in all America and was commonly
referred to as "Black Wall Street." The many banks, theaters,
doctor's offices, and other African American owned businesses were

a source of pride for African Americans in the community and throughout the nation. The economic stability of "Black Wall Street" was shattered in May 1921 during one of the worst pogroms in American history when Tulsa became the first city ever to be bombed from the air. Irving Wallace described the wreckage of the black community in an article on March 13, 1993:

> Whites invaded the black district, burning, looting and killing. To break up the riot, the police commandeered private planes and dropped dynamite. The police arrested more than 4,000 blacks and interned them in three camps. All blacks were forced to carry green ID cards. And when Tulsa was zoned for a new railroad station, the tracks were routed through the black business district, thus destroying it.

There are numerous articles and publications that discuss this sad chapter of American history and they are well worth reading. The GAP Band, a R&B musical group that hails from Tulsa, has kept the memory of this tragic event live. The letters *G, A,* and *P* are the initials of the streets of *Greenwood, Archer,* and *Pine* that were in the heart of the black business district destroyed during the "Tulsa Race Riot."

A similar incident occurred in Rosewood, Florida in January 1923. The black town of Rosewood was completely destroyed by a mob of riotous whites after a white woman claimed to have been assaulted by a black man. The motion picture *Rosewood* which was directed by John Singleton in 1996, documents this tragic episode in African American history.

There is no aspect of life in America immune from the ravages of racism. The specter of white supremacy has also reared its ugly head within the American church. As ministers proclaimed that all humans were children of God from their pulpits, racism prevented blacks and whites from sitting together in the pews. This hypocrisy compelled Richard Allen to establish America's first African American denomination in 1794. True to his cultural leanings, Allen called this institution the *African Methodist Episcopal Church.*

It is often stated that the most racially segregated hour in the United States occurs between 11 AM and Noon on Sunday mornings. European Americans go to a white church and pray to a white God;

African Americans, traditionally go to a black church and pray to a
white God. Within the last decade, however, there has been a
growing movement among African American Christians to
acknowledge the African origins of Jesus the Christ, but I have yet
to see many European Americans embrace this view. These issues
will be discussed in greater detail in Step 10.

In 1992, Pope John Paul II asked God to forgive Christians for
their involvement in the "shameful commerce" of the European
enslavement of Africans. In 1995, during their annual meeting, the
Southern Baptist Convention asked God to forgive the racism they
had condoned throughout their 150 years of existence. Let us not
forget that the burning cross of the Ku Klux Klan represents their
fervent desire to uphold "white Christian traditions."

During the period of African enslavement in the South, white
ministers frequently used biblical scripture to justify slavery. As
recently as May 9, 1996, Alabama state senator, Charles Davidson,
a Republican congressional candidate, used biblical scriptures to
defend the enslavement of Africans. Although Davidson was later
admonished for his views, the relationship between religion and
racism has been examined by numerous individuals and
organizations.

Supposed safe havens for the worship of God, black churches
were often targets of bombings by white supremacists in the 1960s.
African American sanctuaries were not deemed sacred in the past
and their sanctity continues to be disrespected today. During recent
decades, there have been numerous acts of vandalism committed
against African American churches. These attacks have increased
dramatically during the 1990s.

On May 22, 1996, the *Washington Post* reported on a House
Judiciary Committee hearing on church arsons:

> According to Justice Department figures, there have been 28
> arson attacks on African American churches, mainly in the
> South, in the past 17 months. Civil rights groups say as
> many as 45 black churches have been attacked since 1990.

At a Congressional hearing, Deval L. Patrick, Assistant
Attorney General for Civil Rights, testified: "The numbers are
chilling;" "[w]e are facing an epidemic of terror." However,
federal law enforcement officials stated that they had found no
evidence of a widespread conspiracy even though "some incidents

appear related and others have been traced to members of white supremacist groups."

Although several fires were ruled accidental, Judiciary Committee members saw nothing unusual in the fact that an unusually high number of African American churches have been subjected to arson and vandalism. Despite a plethora of horrific attacks, neither the government nor the media has referred to these incidents as terrorist attacks.

It is a sad commentary on the state of this nation when one realizes there is no aspect of life in America exempt from the horrors of white supremacy/racism. The racist social structure was designed to render African Americans mentally, physically, and spiritually subservient to the will of their perceived masters. History teaches that racist organizations and institutions will never change their ideologies until they are forced to do so by the determined will of those who have been oppressed. In the past, whenever changes have been made, they were usually temporarily modifications for political, economic, or religious gains that benefited the "majority" population.

People of African descent must be ever mindful of Francis Cress Welsing's assertion that the driving force behind racism/white supremacy is "white genetic survival." People of European ancestry have historically enacted laws forbidding "racial mixing" because of a basic fear of "genetic annihilation." Scientists have proven that Europeans are genetically recessive, and politicians have enacted legislation to insure that a child borne of a union between a European and a genetically dominant African will never be classified as a white. This reality has been the driving force behind the laws that upheld apartheid, segregation and Jim Crow.

Such laws reveal European commitment to insure their genetic survival in a world dominated by people of color. Racism/white supremacy is an unfortunate reality of life, but its presence should not be used as an excuse for failure. Racism and white supremacy can only be overcome by acknowledging their existence, understanding their operational mode, and formulating plans of action to neutralize their objectives.

Racism works only if you buy into the concept of race and believe in the superficial hierarchical ranking of human beings. White supremacy exists because people of color have been taught to believe in the supremacy of white people and have allowed them to define reality. Racism/white supremacy is a false system that derives its power from the unquestioned support given it by people of color.

Currently, there are numerous propagandists who would have you believe that racism is dead and that America has become a colorblind society. Both statements are completely false. Racism will end only when sexism, greed, and hatred ends and not one second before. Those who claim not to see color are trivializing the ethnic differences that make people unique. Ignoring a person's skin color is a poor excuse for not cultivating humane behavior that allows you to see all people as human and appreciate the divinity that exists within everyone.

It is time for people of African descent to begin empowering ourselves through a change in our consciousness and corresponding changes in our behavior. When these changes are made, they will lead to increased awareness of the power that exists within the individual and the collective group. We have been separated from our sources of power through the use of fear, anger, and miseducation. By using our time judiciously, we can overcome fear, abolish the anger, and empower ourselves with new systems of knowledge and governance.

In concluding this first step, it is helpful for you to do a self analysis of how racism and white supremacy have affected your life. Please set aside some time, on a daily or weekly basis, to conduct the three exercises listed below and record your answers so that you may evaluate and update them over an extended period of time. Do not feel pressured to answer all of the questions in one sitting and, above all, be completely honest with yourself when you do answer the questions.

1. When did you first become aware of racism and how did that initial awareness affect you?

2. Examine the "nine areas of human activity" and list those areas where you have been directly affected by racism/white supremacy.

3. Interview the elder members of your family and discuss the impact that racism/white supremacy have had on their lives. Compare your findings and evaluate the extent to which racist attitudes have changed.

As you record and evaluate your responses, you will become more aware of the presence of racism/white supremacy in your life. As your awareness increases you must not allow yourself to become overwhelmed or intimidated by your findings. This knowledge will help you deal more effectively with the obstacles in your path. Awareness of a problem is often the first step towards developing the ability to overcome it.

References and Suggested Readings

Anderson, Claud. *Black Labor, White Wealth: The Search for Power and Economic Justice.* Edgewood, MD: Duncan & Duncan, Inc, 1994.

Ani, Marimba. *Yurugu: An African-Centered Critique Of European Cultural Thought and Behavior.* Lawrenceville, NJ: Africa World Press, 1994.

Finch III, Charles S. *Echoes of the Old Darkland: Themes From The African Eden.* Decatur, GA: Khenti, Inc, 1991.

Hacker, Andrew. *Two Nations: Black & White, Separate, Hostile, Unequal.* New York: Ballantine Books (Random House, Inc), 1995.

Welsing, Frances Cress. *The Isis Papers.* Chicago, IL: Third World Press, 1991.

The media are incredibly powerful tools that influence society both positively and negatively. During this century, the media have emerged as one of the most effective means of mass communications and manipulation. They mold public opinion, influence social behavior, and play a critical role in determining how people see themselves and how they see others.

Television, radio, and the press are extraordinarily powerful because, through suggestion, they can direct the subconscious minds of their audiences to do the bidding of programmers and publishers. In the hands of racists, these are powerful weapons that have been used to affect the perceptions of reality of both African Americans and other people in society through the manipulation of images and information. Negative images and racial stereotypes, for example, are so commonplace that they are often accepted as legitimate reflections of black life by people who have never met African Americans.

To this end, you must examine all aspects of the media carefully, assess what is being offered, determine what is useful, and consciously discard everything else. This may not be an easy task, but once you become aware of the manipulative nature of the media, you will be able to defend yourself against it.

STEP 2.

Become Aware of the Power of the Media

During my early career as a graphic artist and designer I worked at advertising agencies in Chicago, Illinois and Rosslyn, Virginia. In later years, I have had business dealings with owners, management, and staff of numerous radio and television stations and publishing houses in Illinois, Washington, D.C., Maryland, and Virginia. I have seen advertising and marketing campaigns developed from conception and design to implementation. I have always been intrigued by the interaction of the members of the various creative teams. What fascinated me most throughout this process was that I had an inside scoop on new products and advertisements for them, months before they were introduced to the general public. It was an empowering feeling that generated a sense of tremendous self-worth.

Most creative teams comprise producers, writers, artists, photographers, art directors, photography directors, editorialists, and a host of technicians, who work in concert to sell their ideas to the public. These professionals are responsible for determining every element that is incorporated into any product or advertisement that will ultimately be seen and used by millions of people worldwide. Theirs is a stressful, highly competitive field where loyalties and job security are seldom guaranteed. Creative teams are hired to develop and implement the marketing and advertising ideas of management, and if they don't produce satisfactorily, they are replaced in the bat of an eye.

I can say, with absolute certainty, that everything the public sees and hears has been carefully crafted by minds who are experts in their respective fields. Advertising is a multi-billion dollar industry, and marketing research is constantly upgraded to insure that the advertisements hit their mark. There is minimum tolerance of error in a profession that invests millions of dollars per project and expects profits of 400 percent or more. As one would expect, there are few accidents or coincidences in this business.

If an advertising agency creates a campaign that is particularly successful, the ads will lead to a spate of imitations by competing agencies. There is little originality or shame in a field that thrives on success at any expense.   If this industry also happens to be racist, then white supremacist elements within it will surface in the advertisements created by some and duplicated by others. A careful study of images that have made their way into the American media reveals a pattern of distorted portrayals of African Americans.

Sometimes the degree of racial/white supremacist insensitivity is so blatant that it evokes an immediate reaction, but in many instances the level of racism is almost imperceptible. It is there, but it is subtle and insidious and requires the cultivation of a critical eye for viewers to understand what they are seeing and how it affects them.

The following examples illustrate my point. Analyze them carefully and note the latent images that spring to mind.

During the week of June 27, 1994, shortly after the arrest of O.J. Simpson, both *Time* and *Newsweek* featured photographs of Simpson on their front covers. *Newsweek* used the unretouched Los Angeles Police Department mug shot that ran in dozens of newspapers throughout the country. *Time* used the same photograph but electronically doctored the image, and, according to some, darkened Simpson's face in order to create a more menacing image of a "black" man. The stubble on Simpson's face was enhanced, and the police identification numbers at the bottom of the picture were reduced so as not to compete with the magazine's headline, "An American Tragedy."

There was an immediate public and media reaction to *Time's* "sinister" portrayal of O.J. Simpson. The national criticism was so overwhelming that Jim Gaines, managing editor of *Time,* issued an apology in the July 4 issue:

> . . . it should be said (I wish it went without saying) that no racial implication was intended, by TIME or by the artist. One could argue that it is racist to say that blacker is more sinister, and some African Americans have taken that position in the course of this dispute, but that does not excuse insensitivity. To the extent that this caused offense to anyone, I deeply regret it.

Time   *Newsweek*

With that apology, the issue was dropped, and a lesson was learned. Or so it appeared. Over the years I have observed that whenever racist images in the media are publicly challenged, those responsible for creating the images will deny any racial intent and issue a very generic apology. To this end, Mr. Gaines' response was quite typical of the dominant mindset that runs rampant in American society. The following examples further validate my point.

In September 1993, AT&T published some 300,000 copies of the company magazine *Focus* and distributed copies to their employees worldwide. The publication contained an illustration that portrayed various people in different continents using telephone equipment that was manufactured by AT&T. The illustration depicted Caucasians in North and South America, Northern and Central Europe, all communicating by way of the telephone. However, on the continent of Africa, instead of depicting a Caucasian or African, the artist drew a gorilla chatting gleefully on the phone.

Needless to say, African American employees of AT&T were livid when they saw this humiliating and offensive portrayal of Africans in their company newsletter. They registered their complaints with the corporate offices of AT&T and demanded some form of retribution for those responsible for publishing the illustration.

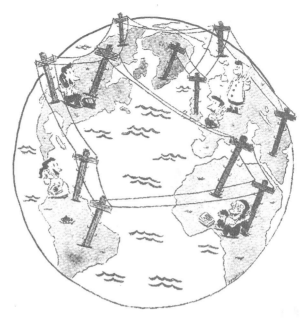

AT&T justice took the form of an apology issued by Marilyn Laurie, senior vice president of public relations, who said she was "appalled and personally deeply sorry about the racist illustration." The editors of *Focus* also issued an apology to, "people of color for an illustration that perpetuates racial stereotypes." They claimed the illustration was "a slip-up in [the] review process between initial sketch and final artwork."

While the editors of *Focus* claimed no personal responsibility for the presence of the illustration, a decision was made to sever all relationships with the freelance artist who drew it. In his defense, the artist countered by saying that he frequently uses gorillas as a trademark in his drawings, and that he had "no intention to hurt anyone."

In the final analysis, neither the editors nor staff at *Focus* saw anything wrong with the characterization of Africans as gorillas. By their own admission, no one caught the "slip-up" during the "review process" because no one was sensitive to the feelings of Africans or their African American counterparts. I believe their inability to see Africans as human beings was a manifestation of their subconscious thoughts of white superiority and black inferiority.

Anyone with an ounce of compassion should have been offended at the sight of seeing a gorilla representing the people of a nation, but when the management of *Focus* was forced to account for their actions, they responded by: 1) denying reality, 2) issuing a pitiful public apology, and 3) offering the illustrator to the African American employees as a sacrificial lamb.

A similar incident received national attention four months later when the African American community was publicly humiliated by a major organization, the Indiana State Medical Association (ISMA). In January 1994, the ISMA distributed 7,000 invitations for its annual legislative reception to its physician members, their guests, and members of the Indiana State Legislature. The invitations included three items: An outer envelope showing the image of a half-naked African, with a bone in his nose, holding a machete; the invitation, which contained an illustration of a monkey eating a banana with the theme of the reception "Jungle Fever" written in bold letters above its head; and an RSVP card imprinted with an image of two Europeans, dressed in safari gear, being cooked alive in a cauldron.

Needless to say, African American physicians and state representatives were outraged when they received their invitations. They lodged numerous complaints against the ISMA for their stereotypical misrepresentation of Africa and African people. They were offended by the portrayal of Africans as cannibals, the reference to Africa as a jungle, and the use of the term *Jungle Fever*, which is a disparaging reference to interracial relationships.

This unexpected response to the invitations prompted Mike Abrams, director of the ISMA, to cancel the reception and issue a public apology to the African American community. Abrams stated, "This is a terrible mistake. I never thought this would be offensive to anyone."

It certainly appears to me that the ISMA, which had no African Americans among its staff of twenty-eight, suffers from the same disorder that causes most people of European ancestry to regard themselves as superior to people of African descent. In some respects, people who are "unaware" of their racist/white supremacist leanings are more dangerous than those who are open and honest with their vile expressions of hate. At least you know where they stand.

Racial insensitivity runs rampant in the minds of people who work in the media, in many institutions, and corporations throughout the United States. Traditionally, European Americans become aware of their racist/white supremacist views only after an offense has been committed and it has been brought to their attention by the offended parties. In most instances, an apology is quickly issued, followed by a denial of any racist intent. However, if these individuals and institutions did not harbor ill thoughts, these incidents would not occur with such frequency. These expressions come from deep within the psyche and are an indication of a sickness that has festered within the souls of Europeans for hundreds of years.

If we examine America's response to the acquittal of O.J. Simpson in October 1995, we find two distinct responses to the verdict fairly evenly split among "racial" lines. While many African Americans were delighted at the sight of a black man receiving justice from the criminal "injustice" system, many European Americans were outraged by a perceived "miscarriage" of justice.

In the weeks that followed, the media played up the apparent perceptual differences between African and European Americans as if the divided consciousness of the society were a new phenomenon and not the consequence of a historical reality that has existed for centuries and continues to play itself out with increasing regularity. Some striking examples of the perceptual differences between African and European Americans can be found in their interpretations of the same subject.

On June 10, 1991, two nationally syndicated publications featured cover stories of the lead actors in Spike Lee's film *Jungle Fever*. One was a European-centered magazine *Newsweek*, and the other was a Negro-centered magazine *Jet*. The differences between the photographs on the two magazine covers reflect the perceptual differences held by most African and European Americans.

The *Newsweek* cover portrayed the Italian American actress, Annabella Sciorra, in a photograph in which she dominates her co-star Wesley Snipes, the African American actor. Snipes' head is shown resting on Sciorra's shoulder, and her hand is placed on his shoulder in a manner that suggests she may be uncomfortable by his presence. This perception is heightened by the fact that neither actor is smiling and written in large letters near their heads are the words "Tackling A Taboo." One can also infer that the secondary headline in the *Newsweek* masthead "Small Cities, Big Crimes: Americas New Murder Capitals" is a not so subtle attempt to associate the image of the black man on the cover with those responsible for the increasing number of homicides in America, thus providing further justification for those who believe that such racial mixing is taboo.

This same couple is portrayed on the cover of *Jet* in a warm embrace and smiling. The photograph shows Wesley Snipes noticeably taller than his co-star. A further comparison reveals another striking difference between the two photos--on the *Newsweek* cover, Mr. Snipes' face is considerably darker and Ms. Sciorra's is noticeably lighter, than their respective images on the *Jet* cover. The earring Snipes wears in his left ear on the *Newsweek* photo is noticeably absent in the *Jet* photo, and even though Snipes is dressed in the typical Euro-American uniform (a suit and tie) his presence is still considered undesirable to European Americans.

Newsweek   *Jet*

An analysis of the two pictures helps to explain the differences between them and the unspoken intentions of each publisher. In most photographs, height denotes power, influence, and superiority. Since males are traditionally taller than females, it is assumed that they are more powerful and superior to them. This is just an assumption which has no basis in reality but is justifiable in a gender-biased society.

The *Jet* cover portrays the typical image of a male and a female. The *Newsweek* cover portrays the unspoken racial and sexual hierarchy that prevails in America. The pecking order in the hierarchy is European male, European female, African female, and African male.

If you were to look at the two magazine covers individually, these subtle differences would probably go unnoticed. However, when you compare them, side-by-side, the subtle differences become quite apparent and somewhat shocking. As you become more aware of the pervasiveness of racism in the media, you will become less shocked and outraged by what you see. You can't hide from the expansive presence of the media, but once you understand how they influence your behavior, you will become better prepared to insulate yourself, and your family, from their negative effects.

We must be mindful of the fact that every image we see on television or film, every publication that we read, and every sound we hear on CD, cassette or radio, has been carefully crafted by specialists and is designed to elicit a specific response from the audience. African Americans must be particularly aware of the negative images of us that have been manufactured in the media over the years. Such media manipulation continues today. Its effects can be controlled by acknowledging its existence and learning to neutralize the negative influences it projects.

African Americans can learn how to hold the media accountable for their actions by examining the actions of other groups who claim to have been offended by the media. In June 1992, President Bush and Vice President Quayle publicly criticized Time-Warner for its distribution of the song "Cop Killer," which was written and performed by rap artist Iced-T. This song, which glorified killing the police, ignited a storm of protest by members of Congress and numerous police groups. By July 28th, Time-Warner succumbed to the pressure exerted on the company and removed the song from future sales of Iced-T's album. This was one instance where discussion of First Amendments rights was superseded by unyielding pressure.

In April 1996, both MTV and VH1 pulled Michael Jackson's video, *They Don't Care About Us,* from their play list because of lingering concerns over two words that were deemed "anti-Semitic." During that same month, Marlon Brando was publicly condemned, and later apologized for having made remarks on *Larry King Live* that were also considered "anti-Semitic."

Do politicians, police officers and Jewish leaders know something about the power of the media that African Americans have yet to realize? Perhaps they understand that disparaging comments made in jest, whether in the lyrics of a song or a conversation, have a potentially lingering effect and must be neutralized before they become ingrained in the consciousness of the society.

If you examine the image of Africans and African Americans in the media, you will find that we are, more often than not, portrayed as savages, clowns, criminals, and social derelicts. Is this an accurate portrayal, or is this how others wish to see us? Why is there no consistent public outcry among African American politicians, clergy, business, and community leaders? Have we accepted these images as a true reflection of our worth as a people, or do we foolishly believe that television, movies, and music have no lasting effects on our lives?

In reality, television, film, and radio are powerful electronic forces that saturate the mind and body with sights and sounds that influence psychological, emotional, and spiritual well-being. It, therefore, becomes extremely important that we balance our viewing and listening habits with sounds, words, and images which soothe our souls and add to our collective worth.

Recommended Activities:

1. Try reading all printed materials through the eyes of the writer, publisher, or art director. Keep in mind that the sentence structure, layout, photographs, and illustrations are all designed to elicit a specific response within you. By becoming aware of these facts, you can monitor how you are being affected by the material and determine the extent to which you wish to be influenced.

2. Apply the same critical approach to television, film, and music as suggested in the activity above. After you've spent several weeks fine tuning your eyes and ears to the messages in the media, begin to designate certain hours of the day, or days of the week, when you will avoid the media altogether. What can you do to fill the void? You can be silent and learn to communicate with your inner self. You can hold meaningful conversations with friends and family members. By the time you have finished reading this book, you will realize that you have many options available to you.

3. This final activity allows you to assume greater control over the media at your disposal. You begin by setting aside time during the day when you will read, view, or listen to materials that you know will enhance your mental, physical, and spiritual well-being. Once you've begun to identify materials that enhance your self-worth, it will become easier to create the environment that best supports your overall development. The benefits you receive from such activities will become noticeable within a matter of days. Your thinking will become clearer and your mind more focused.

References and Suggested Readings

Cohen, Jeff & Solomon, Norman. *Through The Media Looking Glass: Decoding Bias and Blather in the News*. Monroe, ME: Common Courage Press, 1995.

Dates, Jannette L., and Barlow, William, eds. *Split Image: African Americans in the Mass Media*. Washington, DC: Howard University Press, 1993.

Turner, Patricia A. *Ceramic Uncles & Celluloid Mammies: Black Images & Their Influence on Culture*. New York: Anchor Books, 1994.

Note: Marlon Riggs has written, directed, and produced two excellent documentaries on the portrayal of African Americans in the media. They are: *Ethnic Notions* and *Color Adjustment*, and should be available at your local library. Transcripts and video tapes may be obtained from, California Newsreel, 149 9th Street, San Francisco, CA 94103, (415) 621-6196.

Infants are beings, with unlimited possibilities, who are born into the world ready to experience all of the joy and wonder that life has to teach them. They learn to walk, talk, and think by watching and imitating those closest to them. Their home is the first environment that shapes their fragile personalities. What they learn in this setting often determines how they see themselves and how they relate to the world and everything in it. All infants go through this basic rite of passage which ultimately helps to shape their future.

There was a time in the distant past, when those responsible for overseeing the development of youth knew that they were spiritual beings who had taken on human form and had special roles to play in life. They were taught that their thoughts, words and deeds reflected their understanding of their mission in life. Thus, their perceptions of themselves determined their ability to live up to their potential as human beings.

Unfortunately, this blueprint for human development has been unavailable for generations of Africans living in America. Their perceptions of themselves, who they are, and who they are to become have been distorted by the society in which they live. As a result they have been conditioned to believe that they must go outside of themselves in order to find reality. The only way out of this dilemma is for people to learn to reach within and nurture those timeless perceptions of self which will help them construct a new reality.

STEP 3.

Perception Precedes Being . . . You Are Who You Believe You Are

As African Americans we must never forget that our ancestors were compelled, by the letter of the law and the force of the whip, to accept the ideas and beliefs imposed on them by their so-called masters. They were forbidden from expressing their own thoughts and perceptions of the world and were forced to accept the beliefs and behaviors deemed appropriate for them. These steps were taken to ensure the continuation of slavery from one generation to the next. Such social engineering manufactured culturally deficient clones, generation after generation, over the last four centuries. Each successive generation was infected from the time of conception with an ingrained cultural virus that was designed to prevent them from reaching their fullest potential.

But within the soul of African Americans was an unwavering spirit that refused to be dominated. This spirit nurtured a belief, in a receptive host, that there was much more to life than enslavement, poverty, and ignorance. As this spirit grew, the chains of mental bondage slackened, and the consciousness of the enslaved Africans began to expand. Those who nurtured this spirit achieved a state of mental freedom that allowed them to grow beyond the confines of Negrodom. They scaled the walls of Coloredness, found their way through the Blackness, and ultimately rediscovered the African spirit that resided in the center of their souls.

Like Harriet Tubman, these brave ancestors ventured back into "the danger zone" in an attempt to liberate those who remained mentally and physically enslaved to a way of life not of their own design. Freeing the body also meant freeing the mind, and over time the formerly enslaved Africans had to be brought into the light of consciousness. They were taught the value of knowing their true names and reminded that only dogs and slaves were named by their masters. The lessons were simple and yet, very profound.

They were taught that there was no such thing as a *Negro,* that the name and the concept were fabrications of the European mind. They were reminded of the time, in the fifteenth century, when Portuguese sailors kidnapped a group of West Africans and took them to Portugal. When the Africans settled in this new and strange land, they were called *Negroes* by their enslavers. This name was a pejorative reference to the "blackness" of their skin. It has no reference to the home of their birth.

In the centuries that followed, many European nations developed an appetite for stolen land in the new world which necessitated a vast labor force to work the land. Since the European aristocracy and the agents of their God (their popes, priests, and ministers) already regarded Negroes as a race of sub-human, soulless savages, they designated them ideal candidates for permanent enslavement.

The European enslavement of Africans (Negroes) was unlike any previous form of slavery. Without fear of civil or religious reprisals, Europeans condemned Africans to a life of hell on Earth. This scenario set the stage for centuries of kidnappings, murders, and unspeakable atrocities committed against an inestimable number of Africans.

Because of the painful and unresolved memories of our past, many African Americans who continue to encourage their sisters and brothers to remember the struggles of their ancestors are frequently told by others to "get over slavery and forget the past." We must be ever mindful that there has never been a culture that achieved greatness by separating itself from its past. History has shown that wherever culturally-centered people traveled throughout the world, they knew that the retention of their language, culture, philosophy, laws, and god concepts were essential to their survival.

The Europeans who were expelled from Great Britain and forced to seek refuge in North America, attempted in every conceivable way to replicate the culture they left behind. To them the "new world" was to be an extension of the world they left behind. They named the territories *New York, New Jersey* and *New Hampshire* after York, Jersey and Hampshire in "Jolly Ole England." Centuries later, the Eastern seaboard of the United States is still referred to as *New England* and the "unofficial" language of the United States is also called *English* out of respect for the Anglo-Saxon past that is rooted in English culture. No sane people willingly turn their backs on their past. It is only by facing your past that you can accurately perceive reality and determine your destiny. Reality is a pathway to the future, but if that pathway becomes blocked or is partially obscured, then one is destined to wonder aimlessly until the old pathway is found or a new one is forged. African Americans cannot expect to have a sustainable future if we believe we are something that never existed. To that end, the European-created Negro consciousness must die, and we must learn to perceive ourselves in a context which is defined by a new consciousness and not color.

A similar death knoll should be sounded for the perceptions related to the term *Colored* because every person (with the exception of albinos) is colored. We all possess melanin in our skin that protects us from the harmful effects of the sun and gives our skin varying shades of color. The darker your skin, the more melanin it possesses, and the more pigment it produces. This is a basic biological process that is essential for life. Those who live in Africa, a continent whose midsection straddles the equator and is heavily saturated with sunlight, are blessed with darkened skin. This genetic trait has been passed on throughout the millennium to the descendants of Africa who now inhabit more temperate regions of the globe.

When African people ruled the earth, thousands of years ago, black skin was a badge of honor. The color *black* was associated with God and various aspects of divinity. Ausar, the resurrected God/king of ancient Kemet was referred to as "Lord of the perfect black," and the black soil from which he was resurrected was considered sacred. Even the ancient Greeks considered blackness divine. The word *melanin* is derived from the Greek word *melons* which means *black*. Melons is derived from the words, *El* meaning black and *Ann* which is derived from a similar word *amine* which refers to *Amon* or *Amen,* ancient words for God.

Yes, there was a time, thousands of years ago, when black was not only beautiful, but it was also considered divine by all people who possessed, within their skin, the black presence of God. In this respect, everybody was considered colored and some more so than others. It was only after the consciousness of the world was turned upside down that color/blackness became associated with evil and filth, and its antithesis, whiteness, became the metaphor for things good, clean, and holy.

Every black person who speaks the English language experiences a daily struggle to fine dignity in blackness. In 1967, Ossie Davis, the great African American playwright and actor, wrote an article that appeared in the *Negro History Bulletin*, a publication of the Association for the Study of Negro Life and History. The article was entitled "The English Language is My Enemy!" In it Mr. Davis asserted that the language was "infected by racism" and called for a re-examination of our definitions of blackness:

> . . . the word WHITENESS has 134 synonyms; 44 of which are favorable and pleasing to contemplate. . . . Only ten synonyms for WHITENESS appear to me to have negative implications. . . . The word BLACKNESS has 120 synonyms, 60 of which are distinctly unfavorable. . . . When you consider the fact that *thinking* itself is sub-vocal speech— in other words, one must use *words* in order to think at all— you will appreciate the enormous heritage of racial prejudgement that lies in wait for any child born into the English language. . . . Who speaks to me in my Mother Tongues damns me indeed! . . . the English Language—in which I cannot conceive myself as a black man without, at the same time, debasing myself . . . my enemy, with which to survive at all I must continually be at war.

When you think of the synonyms linking blackness with things evil, negative, dirty, or derogatory, a barrage of words and perceptions will flood your consciousness. *Blackmail. Blackball. Blacklist. Black Friday. Black Tuesday. Black death. Black plague. Black sheep.* The list goes on and on.

A *black lie* is a dirty lie but a little *white lie* is acceptable. Even food reinforces negative concepts if you buy into the perceived stereotypes. Black cake is called *Devil's Food Cake* and white cake is called *Angel's Food Cake*. White is angelic, clean, and pure, while black is portrayed as dirty and unholy. If you are aware of these perceptions you will find that they are quite frequently used in the media, as the following examples illustrate.

Since its early beginnings, Benetton, the Italian clothing company has run an often controversial advertising campaign that utilizes the slogan "The United Colors of Benetton." Most of their ads depict the two extremes of the racial spectrum—black people and white people—united in their desire for world peace and in their effort to promote Benetton clothing.

Around 1992, Benetton produced an ad which, like all the others which preceded it, was prominently displayed on billboards, bus stops, and in publications throughout the United States. This particular ad was a simple photograph of two children—a very angelic looking white child, with golden locks like Shirley Temple's, standing next to a black child whose hair was cut into the shape of devilish horns. The subliminal implications and motivation for this photograph were quite clear and intentional. The horns suggest the black child was evil and the flowing hair of the white child suggests she was divine.

In another ad, produced by ABC Television, a similar message was depicted. In the promotionals for a short lived program about two sisters, entitled, "*Good and Evil,*" the good sister was dressed in white and her evil sister was dressed in black. In the logotype for the show the word *good* was written in white letters on a black background with a halo over the letter *G*. The word *evil* was written in black letters on a white background. There were horns protruding from the top of the letter *E*, and a tail extending from the letter *L*. Was this just a random coincidence or part of an ongoing effort to link blackness with the devil, while associating whiteness with things that are good and heavenly?

There are those who sometimes accuse me of being paranoid or "too black," and obsessed with finding racist conspiracies in anything that offends me. I must admit that I am sensitive to such issues because of my background, but I cannot find offensive material where it does not already exist. However, it does fill my heart with great pleasure when I am able to prove a point with crystal clarity, particularly to those who are closest to my heart—like my family. I had such an occasion several years ago when our family threw a surprise birthday party for my mother. My mom received well-wishes from numerous people who were unable to attend her party, including a card from a couple she had known for over twenty-five years.

As fate would have it, this couple happened to be European Americans, and the card they sent was an extremely poor attempt at black humor. It featured a photograph of an obese black transvestite, with horns protruding from its hair, wearing a black dress and holding a black pitchfork. The inside of the card read "Welcome To Birthday Hell," and was accompanied by a handwritten note which read, "This is a terrible card for such a great occasion, but the *devil* made us do it." Needless to say, the card was considered tasteless and offensive to all who saw it, and it was the low point of an otherwise wonderful day.

My mother was at a loss to explain why her "friends" would send such a distasteful card. I reminded her that was how they have been programmed to see us, and they probably didn't give it a second thought. I am quite sure they would never consider sending a similar card to any of their European friends.

I am often reminded of the saying, "It matters not how others see me, what matters most is how I see myself." Thus, I realize that perceptions are critically important for African Americans who live in a society where the very color of our skin is considered evil and dirty. This misconception has had a devastating effect on our psyche for far too long. If we make a conscious decision to refer to ourselves as "Black," then we must continually strive to restore dignity to "Blackness." We must do so by *never* referring to blackness or black people in a demeaning way. Any word that denigrates black people must be stricken from our consciousness, stricken from our thoughts, and stricken from our vocabulary.

We must conduct ourselves in a manner that will create a new definition of blackness in the minds of all people. This consciousness must be instilled in the minds of our youth, and they must be taught to realize that they are representatives of all black people. We cannot afford to allow our youth to "do their own thing." They must be guided by conscious and committed adults who strive to uplift African people.

One of the most striking depictions of blackness in film appeared in Spike Lee's movie *Malcolm X*, in the scene where a young incarcerated Malcolm is encouraged to look up the definition of the words *black* and *white* in the prison dictionary. As the camera pans the definitions, the words fill the screen, and Malcolm's mind is jolted into a state of reality. It is a dramatic moment which impresses upon the viewer, the power of the English language and the power of the media.

Relive this moment by viewing the video tape of the film and watching the scene at least three times. Afterwards, go to a library and secure the definitions of these same words--*black* and *white* -- from at least six different dictionaries. I would recommend the larger volumes because they will have more detailed definitions and list a greater number of synonyms. Once you have compiled these definitions, read them daily for a week and ingrain them in your memory. During the course of that week, make it a point to avoid any negative references to blackness in your thoughts or speech.

Just for fun, try interchanging these concepts when conversing with others. For example:

- Use the word *whitemail* instead of *blackmail* and notice the reaction.

- Never refer to a light skinned person as *fair skinned*. Webster defines *fair* as: "light in color; not dark or dusky; pleasing to the eye; attractive, lovely or beautiful; free from stain, blemish or serious defect." Thus, when you refer to a light skinned person as "fair skinned" you automatically denigrate those of a darker hue.

When you begin to change your perceptions of blackness, you are then in a greater position to influence the perceptions of others. In most instances you will find that creating positive perceptions will help to establish more favorable thoughts and actions and change your behavior for the better. As you modify your thoughts and behavior, you will begin to attract people of a similar mind.

References and Suggested Readings

Akbar, Na'im. *Breaking The Chains of Psychological Slavery.* Tallahassee, FL: Mind Productions & Associates, 1996.

Brown, Tony. *Black Lies, White Lies: The Truth According To Tony Brown.* New York: William Morrow & Co., 1995.

Chideya, Faarai. *Don't Believe The Hype-Fighting Cultural Misinformation About African-Americans.* New York: Penguin Books, 1995.

Every relationship between forces in the universe is affected by the relative power of the opposing forces. When these forces are equal, a state of balance or harmony is established. Growth and forward movement can easily occur in this environment. An imbalance is created then one or more forces are overpowered by another. This leads to stagnation or regression. Therefore, power must be controlled for balance to be maintained and progress to occur.

Knowledge is power. When both are used in tandem, they will forever control the destiny of those who lack one or the other. To this end, if you seek knowledge you must also control the power that accompanies it.

STEP 4.

Information Is Power, But Power Is Nothing Without Control

If we are fortunate, we should have learned early in life that knowledge (information) is power. As we've learned in the previous Step, information (knowledge, words, and perceptions) that is used inappropriately greatly minimizes our base of power. In our quest to acquire knowledge, we must be aware of the sources available to us. We must determine which sources are most valuable. This is a skill that is usually cultivated over time. To this end, experience is the best teacher. Each experience must be carefully evaluated to extract the lessons it would have us learn.

In my ongoing quest to understand the relationship between knowledge, power, and control, I have found two seemingly unrelated examples which illustrate and reinforce this Step. They involve Carl Lewis and Santa Claus.

Carl Lewis, the Olympic track star, is featured in an advertising campaign that was developed for Pirelli, the Italian auto tire manufacturer. Themes of power and control are embodied in each advertisement, and throughout the ads Lewis is depicted as the personification of the product—the Pirelli tire. In each ad, Lewis wears a running suit that is imprinted with a tire tread design, and he performs impossible feats that dramatize how well the tire, and your vehicle, will perform under challenging circumstances. The tag line, which accompanies each ad is, "Power Is Nothing Without Control."

In one ad, Lewis is shown running barefoot on a body of water. The copy beneath his feet reads, "Pirelli tires handle water in ways you've never imagined," which suggests that their product will prevent your car from hydroplaning--skidding on wet surfaces. Similar ads have run in numerous publications and television commercials throughout the country.

On a visit to England several years ago, I was shocked to see a Pirelli advertisement with Carl Lewis that had never appeared in the United States.   On billboards throughout the British countryside, was a photograph of Lewis, in the starting position, wearing red high-heeled shoes. Above his head, in bright red letters were the words, *"Power Is Nothing Without Control"* and beneath his feet was written, "If you're going to drive, drive Pirelli." The inference was obvious, even the best high-performance vehicle will perform poorly with the incorrect tires, or shoes, but the depiction of Lewis, in high heeled shoes with his butt raised up in the air, did more than just raise eyebrows.

Upon further investigation, I discovered that Pirelli made a conscious decision *not* to run that ad in the United States for fear of offending African Americans who might possibly decide to boycott their products. So, to minimize this likelihood, the ad, which was deemed too controversial, ran only in countries where people of African descent had little economic and political influence.

An analysis of this ad and the entire campaign has great significance for advertisers and people of African descent. It teaches us that:

1. Africans in Europe have not amassed the economic power to influence the way they are depicted in the media.

2. Africans in America are major consumers whom advertisers must be careful not to offend.

3. The power of economics, the power of a vehicle, the power of advertising, and the power of knowledge mean nothing if it cannot be controlled for your benefit.

Since knowledge determines a group's economic, social, and political strength, its importance must be understood and controlled if that group is to be empowered, is to compete with, and live harmoniously with other groups. Knowledge is the key to the survival of any group, and it means little if you do not possess the wisdom to utilize it correctly. Information is essential if a person or group is to determine how to act in its own best interests. The accumulation of carefully analyzed and evaluated information establishes a core of knowledge that can develop an even stronger powerbase.

Within the human body, the brain serves as the powerbase that enables us to process information. It determines the extent of our knowledge. Throughout our lives we have been told that the average person uses less than 10 percent of their brain. We have accepted this mental limitation without questioning its deeper significance. Let us consider this statement in the context of an employer/employee relationship. If you owned a company and had employees who worked only 10 percent of the time, and your competitor had employees who performed at 12 percent efficiency, that 2 percent difference would translate into a tremendous profit margin for your competitor.

If our brains work for us, then why should we be satisfied with a maximum output of 10 percent? Should not we desire more of ourselves? How could we ever expect to successfully compete against others who have learned to utilize 12, 15, 20 percent or more of their mental capacity? The answers to this dilemma are quite simple and do not require an expenditure of considerable time or money.

Educators and psychologists have long known about a process by which the average person can increase their brain power. This can actually be achieved by developing one's mental faculties through the application of *cognitive* or *higher order thinking skills*. Thinking enables us to understand what we read, hear, and see. Cognition is the act of clearly knowing or perceiving all data that enter the mind, and it establishes a profound sense of ease or freedom.

Cognition represents a hierarchical thought process that involves three primary thinking skills, the *literal*, the *inferential*, and the *evaluative*. Literal skills help you understand the basic meaning of things. Inferential skills teach you to "read between the lines" and to reason, or *infer*, a hidden truth. Evaluative skills help you formulate opinions and make intelligent decisions after analyzing all available data.

I can best illustrate this developmental process by drawing on my own personal experiences and sharing a story that I'm sure you can relate to. As a child growing up in Chicago, I was taught to believe in the myth (or lie) about a man named Santa Claus. I was introduced to this character by family members who loved me and thought that it was a harmless fantasy. They told me if I were good, this fat, bearded man would bring me any gifts I desired on Christmas Eve.

My belief in this lie allowed me to be manipulated by family members throughout the year because I had interpreted their stories of Santa Claus *literally*. I was told that if I didn't take out the garbage, Santa Claus would not bring me a bicycle, or if I misbehaved in any way, Santa Claus would not stop at my house. Young minds can be easily manipulated and mine was no exception.

As I grew older and reached the *inferential* stage of development, I began to *read between the lines* and raised questions about this stranger who was said to constantly monitor my behavior. I went to the adults in my family with my concerns. I asked them, "How is it possible for Santa to go to every house in the world on the same night?" (The dilemma that this issue poses for adults is that once they tell a lie, they must tell a bigger lie to cover up the previous one, and parents wonder where children develop the habit of lying. They learn from the masters.) In any event, I was told that Santa had helpers to deliver the other children's gifts, but that he was coming to our house personally.

When I was a little older, and realized that we lived in an apartment building without a chimney, I asked my dad, "How is it possible for Santa Claus to bring me my gifts if we don't have a chimney?" I received a very creative response. I was told, "Santa Claus has magic. He'll land on the roof of the apartment with his flying reindeer; he'll snap his fingers and a chimney will magically appear. He'll go down the chimney and leave your gifts, and then go back up the chimney, snap his fingers again, and the chimney will disappear. He'll then fly off to the next house." I believed all of these lies because the people who introduced me to them and reinforced them over the years were people whom I trusted and loved. It was only after I became older and reached the *evaluative* level of thought that I *reevaluated* the story of Santa Claus in an attempt to understand its ramifications on my life.

Once I knew that Santa Claus was a myth, I began to realize that all of the presents that I had received over the years were given to me by my mother and father, grandparents, aunts, uncles, and assorted relatives. They were the real Santa Claus! I then asked myself, "Why would they give someone else credit for gifts that they purchased with their hard earned cash?" The only satisfying answer I received was that they were passing on the same stories that had been passed on to them. They were fed lies as children, which they in turn, fed to their children.

As a parent, I made a commitment to my daughter, and any future grandchildren that the lie and the buck would both stop with me. I explained to my daughter the history of the Santa Claus myth and why we do not celebrate it. She has responded well to the truth.

Santa Claus was originally known as *Saint Nicholas* by the first Dutch settlers in America. The story was embellished by English settlers, who referred to Saint Nicholas as *Santa Claus*. Over the years, St. Nick's appearance continued to evolve, and the image of Santa that we've learned to know and love first appeared in 1863. Currently, many blacks have attempted to assimilate Santa Claus into black culture by portraying him as a person of African ancestry. Africans do not live in the North Pole and it makes no sense to put a black face on a white lie and sell it to our own children.

The moral of this story is that if we've been misinformed in the past, we will probably misinform others in the future unless we consciously break the cycle of mis-information. If we are willing to teach our children to cope with reality, we will soon discover that they are capable of handling the truth with less difficulty than we would imagine.

We African Americans must increase our brain power by developing our cognitive skills. This process begins by reexamining all information that has been presented to us and evaluating it based on our own personal and cultural experiences, our own histories, and our own myths. Myths are essential because they help us determine our own particular way of relating to our world and the people in it. This process teaches us to define our own realities and not be unduly influenced by the realities and myths of others.

The human brain is a muscle which must be exercised by cognitively processing information at the evaluative level. Only then will we be prepared to proceed to the Fifth Step in our program.

Define the following holidays. Look for any relationships that may exist between them, and evaluate their overall significance in the lives of African Americans.

1. Chinese New Year
2. Juneteenth
3. Independence Day
4. Rosh Hashanah
5. Ramadan
6. Columbus Day
7. Thanksgiving Day
8. Kwanzaa

References and Suggested Readings

Barashango, Rev. Ishakamusa. *African People and European Holidays: A Mental Genocide.* Silver Spring, MD: IVth Dynasty Publishing Company, 1983.

Diop, Cheikh Anta. *The African Origin Of Civilization: Myth Or Reality.* Westport, CT: Lawrence Hill & Co., 1974.

Douglass, Frederick. "Fourth of July Oration," A speech delivered July 4, 1852 in Rochester, NY, pp. 637-642 in *African Intellectual Heritage: A Book of Sources.* Asante, Molefi, and Abarry, Abu, eds. Philadelphia, PA: Temple University Press, 1996.

The Earth is inhabited by billions of humans who are subjected to the same forces of gravity, time, and space, whose lives are affected by the elements of Earth, wind, air, and fire. How they perceive these elements and forces is often determined by their geographic location and their cultural orientation. A person living in a desert will relate to the sun and water much differently from someone living on a tropical isle. To this end, the forces and elements of nature, even the plants and animals in the environment, have a profound effect on people's lives and help shape their perceptions of reality.

Thousands of years ago, groups of people lived in relative isolation from other groups. They may have lived at opposite ends of the same country, continent, or planet. The conditions and experiences in their immediate surroundings helped to shape their relationships with each other, their understanding of nature and God, and their relationships with strangers. How the members of a group saw themselves was a legitimate expression of their reality.

As human beings traveled and interacted with other groups, allegiances were formed among those with similar perceptions, and conflicts arose among those who did not see things "eye to eye." In many instances, the losers in any conflict were forced to adapt to the thoughts, behavior, and perceptions of those who conquered them. This did not mean that the perceptions and values of the conquerors were correct, they just possessed the means to impose their values and perceptions on those whom they defeated.

The views and perceptions currently held by millions worldwide, were forged in conflicts and circumstances which occurred hundreds, if not thousands of years ago. The conflicts between Christians and Muslims, and Muslims and Jews, for example, were initiated many generations ago and will continue to affect generations that are yet to be born. Each group has a position which they believe to be correct and are willing to defend that belief to their death.

People have been conditioned to believe in religious causes that they passionately embrace above anything else. This is especially true of African Americans. While religion and spirituality are important issues in the lives of all people, African Americans must become equally impassioned when it comes to rediscovering and retaining their own cultural world view. Such a perspective would allow them to see the world through African eyes and enable them to appreciate that viewpoint. Such a perspective is necessary if Africans are to ever free themselves of the psychological bondage imposed on them by their enslavers generations ago.

STEP 5.

Empower Your Mind . . .
See the World Through African Eyes

As a student in elementary school, I was particularly fond of reading Greek and Roman mythology, especially the fables of Aesop. These stories gave me a greater appreciation of ancient civilizations and helped me understand the extent to which the modern world was indebted to those who studied the mysteries of the universe, life, philosophy, the arts and sciences, thousands of years in the past.

As I grew older, I began to see my childhood heroes through different eyes. I was in high school when I discovered that Aesop was of African descent and that his name was derived from the Greek word *Ethiop*, which meant "burnt face" and referred to the "blackness" of his skin. I also learned that the Greek historian Herodotus stated that the parents of Hercules were Egyptian. I was dumbfounded when I read that *Europa*, the princess for whom Europe was named, was of African ancestry.

After I completed my college studies I began to discover that the ancient Egyptians were really "black" and that many scholars willingly falsified this reality and portrayed the vast majority of them as white. My first trip to Egypt confirmed the historical falsification.

After having traveled to Egypt over a dozen times, I am now convinced that the ancient Egyptians (or Kemiu) had a profound impact on the ancient civilizations of Greece and Rome. I have come full circle, and my eyes are open wide enough to now see the African essence embedded in the accomplishments falsely attributed to Europeans. Thus, my view of the world, and the people in it is now evaluated from a perspective that is much more holistic and culturally centered as the following example illustrates.

There is a very famous statue that was built in the Nile Valley thousands of years ago. It has the head of a man and the body of a reclining lion. Even though this statue was built in Africa by

Africans, we have been conditioned to refer to it by its Greek name, *The Sphinx*. It is important to realize that the word *sphinx* is not the name given this sculpture by its original sculptor. It is a name given it by strangers, thousands of years after its construction. The word *sphinx* does not reflect the symbolic essence of the statue or the nature of the people who created it.

Webster defines *sphinx* as a word of Greek origin which literally means "the strangler." This definition is derived from the story of *Oedipus Rex*, which was written by the Greek playwright Sophocles around 430 B.C.E. In this story, the Sphinx is portrayed as a monster with the head and breasts of a woman, wings of an eagle, and body of a lion. She was perched on a rock near the city of Thebes in Greece and posed a grave threat to its citizens.

This Sphinx posed a riddle to every person who passed her while traveling to or from Thebes, and she strangled anyone who gave her an incorrect response. It was for this reason the Greeks referred to the Sphinx as "the strangler." The Sphinx is also regarded as an enigmatic character often used in the initiation rites of numerous organizations and secret societies. The question posed by the Sphinx is now regarded as the famous *Riddle of the Sphinx*. In this context, this term is used to describe anyone who possesses a deep or mysterious character—a keeper of secrets.

The Riddle of the Sphinx has been expressed in many different ways over the centuries, but the essence of the riddle remains the same. In one version the Sphinx asks: *"What has one voice, and walks on four legs in the morning, two legs in the afternoon, three legs in the evening, and the more legs it walks on, the weaker it becomes?"*

To those with knowledge, this riddle was a test of their higher order thinking ability. It was not meant to be taken *literally*. Those questioned had to *infer* the hidden meaning of the riddle and *evaluate* it based upon their own personal experiences. If they answered correctly, their life was spared, for they possessed the ability to use their higher mind. Those who *failed* this test were deemed unworthy of life and were strangled.

The story of Oedipus Rex (King Oedipus) is regarded as the "definitive Greek Tragedy" and was performed in Athens around 430 B.C.E. In the story, Oedipus was the only person who correctly answered the *Riddle of the Sphinx*. His response was based on his evaluation of the riddle from his own personal viewpoint. This perspective allowed him to give the only reasonable answer, which was, *man*. Because man, in the morning of his life walks on four legs as an infant when he crawls on the ground; in the afternoon of his life, as an adult, he stands erect on two legs, and in the evening of his life, as an elder, he walks with a cane or three legs.

After having been given the correct answer to this riddle, the Sphinx committed suicide by jumping off the cliff, and Oedipus continued his journey to Thebes. Upon his arrival in the city, Oedipus was heralded as a hero for having vanquished the beast which terrorized the Theban countryside. Oedipus was proclaimed King of Thebes and allowed to marry Jocasta, widow of the former King Laius who mysteriously disappeared during a long journey.

King Oedipus and Queen Jocasta produced four children and lived a happy life until a plague devastated Thebes. Oedipus soon learned that he was the source of the city's misery and that he had fulfilled the destiny which was prophesied at his birth. For the man that Oedipus had confronted and killed, prior to his arrival in Thebes, was King Laius, the father who had abandoned him at birth. This revelation also meant that Jocasta was both Oedipus' wife *and* mother, and his children were also his siblings.

Jocasta was unable to live with these events and hanged herself. Oedipus was so overcome with grief that he blinded himself because he no longer wished to see the world that reminded him of his crimes. This myth is the quintessential story of a dysfunctional family and was the source of the *Oedipus complex* theory introduced by the Austrian physician Sigmund Freud in the late 1800s. Freud believed that children possessed an unconscious desire for the exclusive love of the parent of the opposite sex and wished for the death of the parent of the same sex. In later years, researchers used the term *Electra complex* to describe this complex in girls. Electra was a woman in Greek mythology who plotted the murder of her mother.

Thus, an evaluative analysis of the Sphinx, Oedipus, and Freud reveals a historical pattern of distorted family values, murder, and incest. The Greek legacy that Europeans have inherited has been used to describe mental imbalance within the minds of their children and adults. Freud was a remarkable thinker whose perception of society was shaped by his cultural world view. Freud psychoanalyzed Europeans and developed his theories based upon their unconscious feelings that affected their everyday behavior. Many anthropologists have declared that this concept does not exist in non-Western societies and is symbolic of European cultural thought and behavior.

Considering their cultural inclinations, as crazy as it now seems, it was natural for the Greeks to portray the Sphinx as a woman because they believed that females were inferior to males and were inherently evil. The Greeks were also the first "civilization" to legitimize the concept of homosexuality and propagate the belief that the greatest love a man could ever experience was the love of another male. They believed that women were a necessary evil because only they were capable of bringing other males into the world. It goes without saying that these beliefs are not only anti-female, but they also contradict one of the basic tenets of nature, "the balance and harmonious relationship of masculine and feminine energy."

In Africa, we will find the archetype for the Greek Sphinx. We also will discover that it represented an entirely different cultural orientation. One of the African names for this statue was *Her-em-akhet*. It means Heru-on-the-Horizon. This statue has the head of Heru, the son of Ausar, the resurrected God of ancient Kemet, and the body of a reclining lion. Her-em-akhet is located on a plateau at Giza, a city outside of Cairo, Egypt. Giza was referred to as the *akhet*—"the place where the sun rises and sets."

There are some scholars who contend that this statue is over 10,000 years old, but all agree that its meaning is profoundly symbolic. The mind of man is symbolized by the head of Heru, and the lion's body represents the animal nature that rules the body of man. The combination of these two elements symbolizes the process by which every mind can conquer its lower bestial nature if it first cultivates the divine intelligence that exists within the mind. This divine spirit is manifested through Heru who was the son of the world's earliest resurrected God, Ausar. The life of Heru, then, becomes the prototype by which every person is capable of achieving satisfaction on earth--the physical plane of existence.

According to the ancient myth, which originated in Africa over 6,000 years ago, Ausar was the benevolent king of ancient Kemet who was murdered by this brother Set. Aset, the virgin wife of Ausar, mourned the loss of her husband and buried his remains. Because of her undying devotion, the spirit of Ausar visited his wife and impregnated her. Nine months later, Aset gave birth to a son named *Heru*, whose coming was announced by a magnificent star shining in the East and he received gifts from three foreign kings.

Aset protected her son from the army of the king who sought to destroy him. She prepared Heru to fulfill his destiny and reclaim the throne of his father. As an adult, Heru waged a victorious struggle against Set who symbolized the forces of evil.

After Set was brought to justice, Ausar was resurrected from the grave and ruled over the souls of the dead on the Day of Judgment. Ausar was later referred to as the "Lord of Judgment and Resurrection," and Heru was acknowledged as the legitimate ruler of Kemet and called "Lord of the Earth." Aset was regarded as the national symbol of "Divine Motherhood" and established the precedent for the matrilineal determination of kingship.

In an African cultural setting, Her-em-Akhet was a model for African family values. It provided a setting which promoted the ideal of goodness overcoming the forces of evil. The Sphinx, on the other hand, tells the story of Oedipus and a dysfunctional European family. Theirs is a story of incest, murder, and suicide. This one comparison teaches us the importance of evaluating all information from a cultural perspective in order to determine what is truly meaningful in our lives.

In order to develop a greater appreciation of our ancient African civilization and its seldom discussed impact on ancient and contemporary civilization, read Chapters 3 and 4 of my publication, *Nile Valley Contributions to Civilization* and answer the following questions:

1. Explain the historical, cultural, and philosophical differences between Her-em-akhet, the Sphinx, and Adu-hol.

2. Consider the similarities between the stories of Aset and Heru (4,000 B.C.E.) and that of Mary and Jesus (0 A.C.E.). How do you account for their similarities and differences?

3. Consider the origins of the modern alphabet and the fact that the letter "J" wasn't added until about 1600 A.C.E. What are the implications concerning the accurate pronunciation of words and names that now begin with *J* if the references to them date back prior to 1600 A.C.E?

References and Suggested Readings

Akbar, Na'im, *Light From Ancient Africa*. Tallahassee, FL: Mind Productions & Associates, 1994.

Asante, Molefi, and Abarry, Abu, eds. *African Intellectual Heritage: A Book of Sources*. Philadelphia, PA: Temple University Press, 1996.

Browder, Anthony T. *Exploding The Myths Vol. 1: Nile Valley Contributions To Civilization*. Washington, D.C.: The Institute of Karmic Guidance, 1992.

Carruthers, Jacob H. *Mdw Ntr: Divine Speech: A Historiographical Reflection of African Deep Thought From The Time of the Pharaohs to The Present*, Lawrenceville, NJ: Red Sea Press, 1995.

Diop, Cheikh Anta. *Civilization Or Barbarism: An Authentic Anthropology*. Brooklyn, NY: Lawrence Hill Books, 1991.

Hilliard, III, Asa G. *The Maroon Within Us: Selected Essays on African American Community Socialization*. Baltimore, MD: Black Classic Press, 1995.

Part Two

BODY

All human life is significant because it possesses a spirit that animates the soul hosted in the body. Everybody has a soul. No two souls are alike, and the bodies that contain them comprise complex systems that must be carefully maintained and properly balanced for harmony to exist within the mind, body, and spirit.

For a mind to be controlled, it must believe three things: that it functions independent of the body, that all bodies operate the same, and that the spirit exists outside of the body. When falsehoods are accepted as fact, they allow a person to willingly abuse their body. When a person's body is defiled, it will ultimately lead to the degradation of the mind and spirit. When people truly seek to know their body, one of the simplest mysteries of life will be revealed to them. They will come to understand that the body is the temple that houses a soul and spirit from the Creator who expresses itself through the thoughts and ideas that are generated within the mind. If the sanctity of this temple is honored as the body progresses through various stages of development, the mind will be able to manifest the divine talents that exist within, and humanity will be the beneficiary of this relationship.

All humans have special needs that vary according to age, sex, and ethnicity. These special needs make them different from one another but not necessarily better. What nourishes one body may be harmful to another. A group which lives in an Arctic environment has nutritional needs that are different from a group that lives in a tropical environment. When the specific needs of a group are not met, they will be incapable of cultivating their divine talents and will engage in a passionate dance with disaster.

It has been said that a chain is only as strong as its weakest link. To that end, it might also be stated that a group is only as strong as its weakest habit. It does little good for African Americans to engage in a struggle for mental or spiritual liberation if their minds and souls are contained in a body that serves them poorly. You must become fully aware of the needs of your African body and the steps that must be taken in order for you to live a truly meaningful life.

(Note: This statement will apply for Steps 6, 7 and 8).

STEP 6.

Become Aware of the Uniqueness
of Your African Body

The human body is a wonderful instrument that undergoes constant change throughout its lifetime. The needs of an infant are profoundly different from those of an adolescent or adult. A woman who is pregnant has physical needs that change when she begins to breastfeed her child. Her physical needs continue to change as she ages. Change is the one consistent reality we will meet as we travel between the posts that mark the beginning and ending of our life. How well we prepare for those changes, or respond to them when they occur, will ultimately determine the quality of our life.

As we grow older, we become aware of general guidelines of physical development determined by age and sex. The physical needs of most children are similar until they reach puberty when the biological development of males and females diverge. Because we live in a male-dominated society that portrays females as the "weaker sex," we have been conditioned to downplay the value of females. Most of our perceptions of health and medicine were derived from the teachings of physicians who, for the most part, have been European and male. In some instances, their regard for their female counterparts has been less than admirable.

During the 1700s, European researchers noted that females were more inclined to commit suicide, murders, and other acts of violence during menstruation. Physicians speculated that the uterus was the source of this female problem. They referred to this state of uncontrolled emotional excitability as *hysteria*, which was also linked to a host of other physiological disorders in women. The medical response to this dilemma was to perform a *hysterectomy* and "remove the source of the hysteria."

Hysteria is derived from the Greek word *hystera* which refers to the uterus or womb. "Hysterectomy" comes from the Greek words, *hystera*, and *ektome*, which mean "to cut out." In hindsight, it took medical scientists almost 200 years to discover that hysteria was hormonal and more closely related to a chemical imbalance caused by the ovaries and had little to do with the uterus. This condition is now called *PMS* (Pre-Menstrual Syndrome) and has been successfully treated with drugs, hypnosis, and or psychotherapy. In a March 27, 1995 *Newsweek* article, "The New Science Of The Brain: Why Men and Women Think Differently," neurologists acknowledged the existence of profound physiological differences between the way men and women *think* and *process information*. The data showed that both hemispheres of the brain are connected by a bundle of nerves called the *corpus colossum*. It appears that the female brain possesses an enhanced "interface" between the left and right brain that allows it to process more information faster than the corpus colossum in the male brain.

There has also been an increased awareness of the role that genetics play in determining an ethnic group's susceptibility or immunity to disease. This reality has led some nations to conduct research in the development of biological weapons which are "ethno specific." In *A Higher Form of Killing (The Secret Story of Chemical and Biological Warfare)*, Robert Harris and Jeremy Paxman, address this issue in great detail.

Modern science is now capable of exploiting the minute differences that distinguish males from females and one ethnic group from another. It should come as no surprise that there are also profound neurological and physical differences between Africans and Europeans. Anyone who has ever given blood or has had a need for an organ transplant knows that there are genetic traits that divide people into specific categories classified by sex, blood type, and ethnicity.

The complexities of the human body are truly amazing but we must not overlook those traits that make one group of people distinct from another. Most people of African descent have genetic differences which give us physiological advantages over people of European ancestry. For example:

- Africans contract skin cancer at rates significantly lower than Europeans.

- The rate of osteoporosis is noticeably lower in elderly African females than it is in elderly European females.

- A comprehensive study of African infants has shown that they are able to sit upright, walk, talk, and respond to external stimuli, months earlier than their European counterparts.

These facts point out just some of the specific advantages that are directly related to possessing a highly melaniated body. The scientific community has been aware of such facts for decades, but they have not been made readily available to the general public. I believe one of the reasons researchers have not been more forthcoming is because they are primarily concerned with European interests.

This situation places an extra burden of responsibility on African American researchers and scientists who run the risk of being ostracized for focusing on our own health concerns. Additionally, it places an extra responsibility on the African American community who must also become aware of certain physiological disadvantages that confront them. For example:

- Many Africans have a lactose intolerance that prevents them from digesting dairy products as easily as Europeans do.

- The stress of living in a racist environment has a profound effect on a person's health and has been linked to a higher rate of strokes, hypertension, and heart attacks.

- Africans who smoke marijuana, shoot heroin, snort cocaine or smoke crack cocaine are prone to get higher faster and remain addicted longer than their European counterparts. This is attributed to the similarity in the chemical structure of the aforementioned street drugs and the melanin in the African body. All of these drugs are alkaloids that chemically merge with melanin and alter its functions with serious consequences.

If Africans are to live more meaningful and productive lives, we must become keenly aware of our strengths and weaknesses. There are certain substances that can be consumed by Europeans but are detrimental to Africans. We must identify such substances and avoid them. Conversely, we must also identify and ingest substances that optimize the performance of our African bodies. If we remain ignorant of the hereditary traits that are unique to African people, we will ultimately abuse our bodies and suffer needless and prolonged illnesses.

For those African Americans who are unsure of their "racial identity" because of their mixed heritage, I remind them of the "one drop" rule which has been in effect in America for over 200 years. As long as a person had 1/64th of black blood, they were considered nonwhite. This issue is of growing concern in the

European American community but for of a different reason. Generations ago thousands of African Americans passed for white in an attempt to escape the ravages of enslavement and discrimination. Today, many of their "white grand children" are born with sickle cell anemia. This situation has prompted the Center for Disease Control (CDC) to encourage white parents to test their new borns for Sickle Cell.

In the decades before the end of segregation and discrimination, African Americans were forced to seek medical treatment in Negro hospitals and were attended by Negro physicians and nurses. In many instances, these clinicians were more sensitive to the needs of their patients--for obvious reasons. Now that we are free to be treated by any health care provider in any medical facility, I would strongly advocate seeking out African Americans whenever possible. They are deserving of our support.

All health care providers work for their patients and are obligated to deliver the best service possible. Patients also have a responsibility to become more involved in the maintenance of their own health. Numerous medical surveys indicate that increased death and illness among African Americans could be greatly reduced if they took better care of themselves and sought early medical treatment for their ailments.

Take time out to assess your health status and consult a physician if you have not done so within the past twelve months. One of the reasons African Americans have a high mortality rate is due to delay in seeking medical attention. You should always strive to maintain an optimal state of health by consuming a proper diet and regular exercise.

There is a growing number of physicians who are turning to alternative sources of healing that emphasize the whole person-- mind, body, and spirit. John T. Chissell, M.D., is such an individual. He is the author of *Pyramids of Power! An African Centered Approach to Optimal Health.* His book is chock full of invaluable information and suggested readings. Dr. Chissell has also produced an audio cassette, *Affirmations For Optimal Health, Harmony and Relaxation.* These items are intended for people of African ancestry and may be ordered from:

Positive Perceptions Productions, P.O. Box 31509, Baltimore, MD 21207-8509 (Phone: 410/448-4352).

References and Suggested Readings

Africa, Llaila O. *African Holistic Health.* Brooklyn, NY: A&B Books Publishing, 1983.

Africa, Llaila O. *Nutricide: The Nutritional Destruction of the Black Race.* Beauford, SC: Golden Seal, 1994.

Afua, Queen. *Heal Thyself For Health & Longevity.* Brooklyn, NY: A&B Book Publishers, 1992.

Chissell, John M.D. *Pyramids of Power! An African Centered Approach To Optimal Health.* Baltimore, MD: Positive Perceptions Productions, PO Box 31509, 1993.

Villarosa, Linda, ed. *Body & Soul: The Black Women's Guide to Physical Health and Emotional Well-Being.* New York: HarperCollins Publishing, 1994.

(Note: These References and Suggested Readings are applicable for Steps 6 and 7).

STEP 7.

Develop Cultural and Holistic
Approaches to Health

The quality of our health is influenced by many factors: finance, sex, culture, and ethnicity. Of profound significance is the degree to which the European model has been used as the standard against which all others are measured. This is exemplified by the phrase "in the pink" which refers to a person of European ancestry who is in good physical condition. "In the pink," refers to the observable phenomena of oxygen-rich red blood coursing through the arteries beneath pale "white" skin. The rules of basic color combinations still hold true whether it is in an art class or the body: red and white still make pink.

Because of the high concentration of melanin present in the skin of Africans, we can never be *in the pink*. Our skin is not as translucent, and it is much more difficult to ascertain when we become flushed. Consequently, we must use a different criteria to observe and express the health status of African people.

Granted, all humans bodies have many common traits and these similarities should not be overlooked. Deepak Chopra, M.D., author of *Ageless Body, Timeless Mind,* informs us that the cells in all of our bodies undergo 6 trillion reactions every second of every day. He describes this miraculous process of cellular regeneration with profound clarity:

> The skin replaces itself once a month, the stomach lining every five days, the liver every six weeks, and the skeleton every three months . . . By the end of this year, 98 percent of the atoms in your body will have been exchanged for new ones.

Our bodies comprise many systems: reproductive, circulatory, digestive, and others, that must all work individually and collectively to achieve the state of wholeness we call health. Many Western-trained healers, physicians, psychiatrists, dentists, and others, are just beginning to acknowledge holistic approaches to health that have been practiced in other cultures for thousands of years.

Traditional African healing is holistic and is based on the healers' understanding of the interrelationship of a person's mind, body, and spirit, and how they all interact with nature and the universe. The European, or Western approach of health, is predicated on the belief that the mind is separate from the body, and the soul is nonexistent because it cannot be seen, weighed, or measured. Such an approach to medicine considers the body to be unaffected by universal forces.

Most health care providers are unaware that the *caduceus*, the universal symbol of the medical profession, actually symbolizes an ancient holistic approach to medicine. This symbol is of African origin and it represents the physical, mental, and spiritual components of the human body as defined by ancient African priests, scientists, and physicians. If you were to ask your physician the meaning of the caduceus, I would hazard a guess that nine out of ten would be unable to give you a satisfactory answer. Their inability to do so is not a reflection of their ability to dispense medical advice, it merely indicates their lack of knowledge of African history.

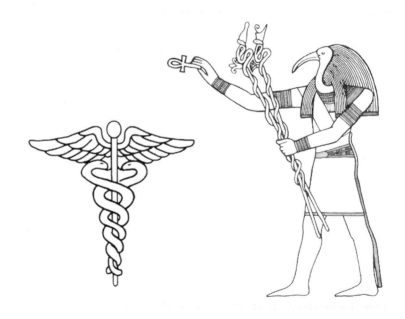

The caduceus is a modification of a Kemetic symbol that was associated with healing. The caduceus represents the human body and the systems within the body that must be properly maintained and balanced for good health. It comprises a staff with two serpents intertwined around it and a globe on top of the staff with wings projecting from both sides.

The globe represents the brain, and the staff symbolizes the spinal column, which is connected to the base of the brain. The two serpents represent the flow of oxygen, blood, and nutrients from the heart to the entire body via the circulatory system. The wings represent the state of *ease* or *equilibrium* that is created in the body when the energy flow within the circulatory and nervous systems is unimpeded. If the flow of energy becomes impaired, a state of *dis-ease* occurs, and the body becomes susceptible to illness at the sight of the blockage.

The origin of the caduceus can be traced back to the African civilization of Kemet in the Nile Valley. At the temple of Seti I (*c.* 1300 B.C.E.), there is a wonderful relief carving of *Djhuiti,* the African Netcher, or God, who was associated with the science of medicine. Djhuiti holds, in his left hand, two staffs with a single serpent intertwined around each. Each staff and serpent represent the upper and lower geographical regions of Kemet. They also represent the upper and lower regions of the human body.

In this carving, Djhuiti is also holding, in his right hand, an *ankh* (the symbol of life) which he extends to the nostrils of King Seti. Seti receives the "breath of life" and the promise of health and well-being from Djhuiti, the master healer. Djhuiti was also regarded as the mythological teacher of Imhotep who is recorded in history as the world's first physician. Imhotep was a multidisciplinarian who lived in Kemet around 2630 B.C.E., and practiced medicine over 1900 years before the birth of Hippocrates, the reputed "Father of Medicine," in Greek history.

Djhuiti was acknowledged in Kemet as the God of science, medicine, mathematics, and writing. He was also associated with measurement and was considered a master of the spoken word. Djhuiti was regarded as the divine articulator of speech and possessed the ability to bring objects into existence via the spoken word. He was referred to as *Thoth* by the early Greeks who visited Kemet.

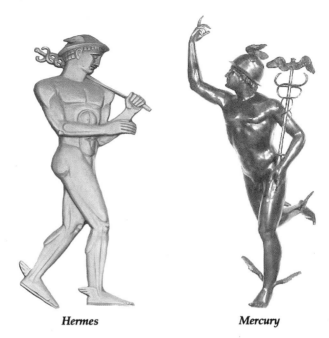

Hermes   *Mercury*

The word *thought* was derived from the Greek word *Thoth* which referred to the cognitive abilities of Djhuiti, the Kemetic God of divine speech. Let us not forget the words of Ossie Davis who reminded us in Step 3 that "...thinking...is sub-vocal speech..."

Much of the medical and scientific terminology used today originated from the Romans and Greeks who acquired some of their concepts from the people of Kemet. When Kemet was conquered by Greece in 332 B.C.E., it was renamed *Egypt*. After this conquest, many elements of Kemetic science, philosophy, and culture were infused into Greek culture and, over time, were attributed to the Greeks. One such example was the Hellenization of Djhuiti who became known to the Greeks as *Hermes, the God of Medicine*. Greek depictions of Hermes show him carrying a staff with two serpents intertwined around it. This instrument was called *The Staff of Hermes* and eventually became known as the *Caduceus*.

When the Romans conquered the Greeks, and gained control of Egypt in 30 B.C.E., they integrated elements of Greek culture into their society. Subsequently, the Greek god Hermes became known to the Romans as *Mercury, the God of Medicine*. The Roman god Mercury assumed all of the attributes of Hermes, and *The Staff of Hermes* was referred to as *The Staff of Mercury*. With this background it is apparent, even to the most feeble mind, that Mercury was a Roman version of the Greek Hermes, and both were European versions of Djhuiti, the Kemetic god of medicine. The Roman god Mercury symbolized swiftness of thought and motion. He was depicted wearing wings on his feet and hat. These attributes were also associated with the silver-white metallic chemical element of the same name which is called *quicksilver*. In Roman mythology, Mercury was the name given to the planet nearest the sun. As a matter of fact, all of the names currently used to identify the planets in our solar system were derived from the names of Roman gods, whose identities were previously associated with Greek gods. Thousands of years earlier, these same planets were given African names by astronomers in Kemet.

Mercury was synonymous with speed as it is the planet which travels the fastest around the sun. It completes its orbit in just eighty-eight days. The sun was a symbol that represented God to the ancients in Europe and Africa, and it also symbolized the human mind. In Roman mythology, Mercury was called the *messenger of the Gods*. Since the planet Mercury has the quickest orbit around the sun, this speed also symbolizes the ability of Mercury to quickly disseminate messages from the Sun (God) to the other planets in the solar system (the lesser gods).

This symbolism also served as a profound metaphor for a specific activity that takes place within the human body. Modern neurologists view the brain as the central processing computer that coordinates myriad functions within the body. To ancient scientists, this same process was expressed much more poetically. To them, the brain was the sun within our "internal solar system." The chemical messages from the brain (our sun) were transmitted throughout the body via the circulatory system, onto the other organs (or planets) within the body. These chemical messages are called *hormones* and they direct the activity of specific organs and tissues in the body. The word *hormone* was derived from the Greek word *Hermes*, who had the dual responsibility, as did Mercury, of being the God of Medicine and Messenger of the Gods.

Hormones are chemical substances produced in one area of the body which cause an effect in a different part of the body. The *World Book Encyclopedia* states that:

hormones serve as a means of communication among various parts of an organism. They act as 'chemical messengers' that help these parts function together in a coordinated way. The word *hormone* comes from a Greek word that means *set in motion* . . . hormones control such body activities as growth development, and reproduction. . . . If an organism fails to produce the proper kind or amount of hormones, serious disturbances—or even death—may result.

Most hormones in the body are produced by organs called *endocrine* (ductless) glands. They secrete hormones into the bloodstream, which distributes them throughout the body. When a hormone arrives at its designation, the specific organ or tissue it affects, it causes specific actions to occur. The pineal gland, which was once considered a *vestige* organ, is now acknowledged as the "master gland" in the body. It secretes hormones that affect the secretion of hormones in the other endocrine glands.

Throughout the ages, the actions of the pineal gland have been associated with Djhuiti, Thoth, Hermes, and Mercury. Each mythological figure was affiliated with the science of medicine and considered to be a messenger of God and bearer of divine gifts—thought and speech. Modern health care professionals have retained the signs associated with the field of medicine, but many are unaware of their deeper symbolic meaning.

Within traditional African societies and in numerous cultures throughout the world, people still celebrate adolescence--the transition of a child into adulthood that begins at puberty. This period is marked by an onslaught of hormonal activity that produces dramatic physical changes in the bodies of males and females. A rite of passage was usually initiated in the thirteenth year of life and prepared youth for the beginning of a mental, physical, and spiritual metamorphosis into adulthood. A rite of passage was essential if youth were to learn how to function as adults and sustain the harmony, integrity, and stability of the village. The idea of an entire village raising a child is not a worn out cliché, it is a fact of life.

The attributes of Djhuiti, and the meanings associated with Thoth, the caduceus, Hermes, and Mercury have been lost over the ages, but the process they represent will continue to exist as long as there are humans on earth. When people are separated from the deeper meaning of life, they suffer many hardships. Those who have forgotten the importance of rites of passages will produce children to whom life has no value or meaning. Not only has the significance of sacred rituals been forgotten by Africans in communities throughout America over the years, critical values have been lost at a time when they are needed most. In these modern times, single-parent families are becoming the norm and, extended families are practically nonexistent. The closeness of the village no longer exists. Children are producing children at an increasingly younger age and they lack the life skills necessary to pass knowledge on to the next generation. To further compound matters, we have witnessed a continual decline in the age that youth reaches puberty. Today, it is not uncommon for a female to begin her menstrual cycle as early as 8 or 9 years of age. Research indicates that this change, as well as the tremendous increase in the size of our children, closely parallels the growth of the fast food industry over the past thirty years.

Almost two generations of children have been raised on fast food. The chickens, cows, and pigs that are served in most restaurants were previously fed a diet of growth hormones in an attempt to minimize the time span between their birth and slaughter. The same growth hormones fed to livestock continue working inside the bodies of youngsters long after they have eaten their "happy meals." These chemical substances now wreak havoc within young bodies and are accelerating the onset of puberty.

It would not surprise me to see future government regulations that require warning labels on all fast-food products to advise parents of the risks associated with allowing their children to ingest hormone-laden food. I am reminded an old axiom, "You are what you eat." In light of this fact, I feel that all of our children deserve a break--today and everyday.

Children deserve to be raised by thoughtful adults who will protect them as youth and prepare them for adulthood. If it takes a village to raise a child, it takes culture to sustain a village. Where there is no culture, there is no village, and the people will perish.

STEP 8.

Become Aware of Your Mind/Body Relationships

As wonderful as our bodies are, they are incapable of distinguishing between reality and fantasy. Our body is designed to respond to the messages that flow through it from the mind. The brain is an elaborately designed command center that directs the flow of billions of electrical impulses and the secretion of powerful hormones that direct every activity in the body.

The functioning of cells, tissues, muscles, and organs are all directed by activity in the brain and influenced by thoughts within the mind. There is a newly emerging field of medicine in Western science that is devoted to researching the links between the mind and body. Numerous physicians and scientists, at some of the top rated universities and hospitals in America, are now acknowledging the role that the mind plays in healing the body and preventing illness.

Of particular importance is understanding the role that stress plays in causing illness within the body. Stress and fear cause many adverse physical reactions within the mind and body. It does not matter if the stress or fear is self induced or the by-product of external circumstances, the body always reacts negatively to these forces. When the body is exposed to a life-threatening or stressful situation, it responds by initiating an emergency procedure referred to as the *fight or flight syndrome*. Within fractions of a second, fear induces a physiological response, which prompts the adrenal glands to pump epinephrine into the blood system. This chemical flows throughout the body to the muscles and provides them with, short-term, super human strength. The body is now prepared to either fight or run for its life.

There have been numerous accounts of mothers who have lifted cars off of a child who was being crushed, or injured soldiers performing heroic acts during a heated battle. Stressful situations sometimes cause ordinary people to do extraordinary things.

Have you ever been involved in a life threatening situation? Do you recall how you responded to it? What is important is to understand how that event continued to affect you.

When a stressful situation ends, your body returns to normal, but the memory of that event is stored in your mind forever. If you were to relive that stressful situation in your mind, just by *thinking* about it, your body will respond by secreting the same stress hormones as when the event actually occurred. Your heartbeat and temperature would increase as your body responds to a situation that exists only in your mind. In effect, your body is sometimes incapable of distinguishing between thoughts that are real and thoughts that are memories of real events.

Stress and fear wreak havoc on your mind and body, and their cumulative effects cause long-term damage. Therefore, you should always be aware of the nature of your thoughts and their ability to induce changes within your body. These changes can also affect others around you. The following story underscores the dangers of unguarded thoughts:

> A woman, breast feeding her child, was thinking about a argument that she had earlier in the day with her mate. As the child nursed, the woman's body, in response to her thoughts, began secreting adrenaline into her circulatory system. Minute amounts of adrenaline made its way into the mother's breast milk and was ingested by the child who died of adrenaline poisoning.

Our thoughts exert a powerful force over our bodies. They trigger the release of hormones that flow into our blood system and affect us in myriad ways. Our thoughts are capable of influencing our internal organs, our behavior, and the behavior of others. When we focus our thoughts, we gain power. That power can be used to enhance our lives or make them worse.

Dean Ornish, M.D., one of several physicians interviewed by Bill Moyers in the publication, *Healing and The Mind*, advises:

> . . . when you can focus energy, you gain more power, for better and for worse. For example, if your mind is focused, then its effect on the body becomes enhanced, also for better or for worse. Unfortunately, in our culture we tend to have our minds most focused when we are angry, upset, afraid, or worried. You know, someone once said that anger

wonderfully concentrates the mind. That's really true, but that form of concentration can have a negative effect. Your heart rate goes up, your blood pressure goes up, the arteries in your heart may begin to constrict, and the blood may clot. But we can use that same principle in a healing direction rather than in a harmful one by learning to concentrate mental energy.

The idea of focusing the mind in a positive, healing direction is reflected in the ideals of *Karmic Guidance* which I have espoused in my writings and lectures for many years. I believe that our thoughts emit a powerful force that attracts to us those things that we focus our attention on. I believe we are capable of manifesting health and prosperity in our lives if we understand who we are and what we are capable of doing with our bodies and minds. I use two demonstrations to illustrate this truth.

The first demonstration involves a device called an *Energy Sphere* which is about the size of a ping pong ball. Inside the Energy Sphere are two batteries, a small light emitting diode, and a circuit board that contains a sound chip. On the exterior of the Energy Sphere there are two metal strips that are connected to the positive and negative terminals of the batteries inside. This little device was designed to demonstrate the flow of electrical energy through the human body.

Placing a finger on each of the two metal strips completes an electrical circuit that causes the Energy Sphere to glow and hum. Your body becomes a conduit for the flow of electrical energy. If you lift a finger off of the metal strip, the electrical circuit is broken and the sphere ceases to glow and hum.

This demonstration is even more dramatic with a group of four to ten people holding hands in a circle. If two people in the circle place a finger on each of the sphere's metal strips and then hold hands with the person next to them, they will complete the circuit and the sphere will glow and hum. The circuit remains complete and flows from one person to the other as long as their hands are held. If one person releases his grip, the circuit is broken and the sphere will cease to function.

This simple presentation reinforces the fact that energy flows through us, singularly and collectively. The human body is capable of transmitting and receiving various forms of energy. The Energy Sphere is designed to illustrate the flow of electrical energy, but other forms of energy, such as thoughts and emotions, are being transmitted and received all of the time. Thoughts and feelings generated within the mind are nothing more than electrical impulses that are governed by the same laws as electricity. They may be more difficult to see and measure, but they exist just the same.

Thoughts, like other forms of energy, can be used for constructive or destructive purposes. We should always know what we are doing when dealing with any electronic device and it should always be properly grounded. All electronic appliances come with instructions that teach you how to maximize your use of the product. It is most unfortunate that the human mind, which is responsible for creating all of the devices in our environment, does not come with similar instructions. As a result, many people spend their lives misusing their energies or never developing their full potential.

Just because information has not been made available to you does not mean that it does not exist. If you learn to cultivate the desire for knowledge, your mind will attract it to you. You will then have to analyze and evaluate that information before you can use it correctly.

My second demonstration helps to illustrate this principle. It is a simple exercise that shows how four people, working collectively, can unify and direct their thoughts to accomplish a seemingly impossible task.

The demonstration requires one person to sit comfortably in a chair with two people standing behind each shoulder, and with two people standing at right angles to each knee. All four persons are instructed to fold their hands leaving only their two index fingers extended. The couple standing by the seated person's knees is instructed to place their index fingers under each knee. The other couple is instructed to place their index fingers under the seated person's armpits. The objective is for all four persons to lift the seated individual out of the chair by using just two fingers each.

The first time this effort is attempted it will be unsuccessful. It is done merely to illustrate the difficulty of the task. The four persons are then instructed to each place their left hand over the seated person's head. The hands are placed one after the other with a space of one inch between each hand. When the left hands are in position the procedure is repeated with each right hand.

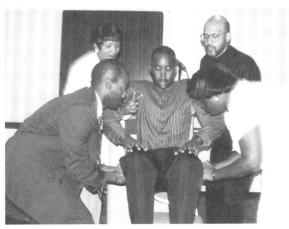

With both hands now placed over the head of the seated person, those standing are instructed to visualize themselves *lifting* the person out of the chair. After a minute, this vision becomes fixed in the minds of those standing. They are then instructed to remove their hands, one by one, and reassume their previous lifting position. When the command is given, the four people will now be able to lift the person out of the chair with ease.

This demonstration is effective the second time it is attempted because the energy, which was harnessed while the hands were placed over the head of the seated person, was directed during the visualization exercise. In other words, the energy which flowed through the hands of the four people was synchronized with the energy of the person sitting in the chair. When the directive was given to *visualize* the person being lifted out of the chair, their bodies responded by producing the energy necessary to make the request possible.

There certainly is nothing magical or deceptive about this demonstration. It is a simple method of illustrating the untapped powers that exist within every person. If we evaluate the principles behind both demonstrations, we will see direct linkages between the human body and the caduceus.

As demonstrated in the exercise with the Energy Sphere, energy flows through the human body. The left hand is regarded as feminine and receives energy. The right hand is regarded as masculine and transmits energy. This energy also flows through the spinal column, into the brain, and in and out of the crown of the head. This metaphysical concept is embodied in the symbolic representation of the caduceus. The two serpents of the caduceus represent the positive and negative (masculine and feminine) flow of energy, which moves horizontally throughout the body. The staff and globe represent the spinal column and brain and the vertical flow of energy through the body.

Every person possesses at least three types of power: *physical power*, which can be seen when we engage in any type of movement and *mental power*, which is expressed through the physical whenever we move, talk, or produce things. There is also a *spiritual power* we all have that inspires the mind to set in motion activities that are performed by the body. This spirit, mind, and body relationship functions within every person whether he or she is conscious of it or not. This relationship has been depicted metaphorically, metaphysically, and symbolically throughout the ages. We have seen these depictions most of our life, but we have not been taught their meaning or how to identify them.

Here are a few examples for you to consider. We have all seen paintings of Jesus The Christ in churches, on fans, and in Bibles. In many of these paintings Jesus is depicted holding His left hand to His heart and extending His right hand. This pose symbolizes the flow of spiritual energy through the body of Christ—the Anointed one. In these paintings, the left hand of Jesus receives the energy from his heart (which is a symbol of love) and the right hand transmits His energy/love to you.

People engage in a similar ritual when they are called to take the witness stand in court. As they are sworn in, they are instructed to place their left hand on the Bible and raise their right hand. When they make a pledge or affirm their allegiance to a nation or an organization, they are asked to raise their right hand and affirm to faithfully *discharge* their duties. The symbolism inherent in these rituals reflects the unspoken belief that energy is received with the left hand and discharged with the right.

The left side of the body, which is feminine, is controlled by the right hemisphere of the brain which is also considered feminine. The converse is also true for the left hemisphere of the brain and the right side of the body. The right brain processes abstract thoughts, symbols, metaphors, sounds, and colors. The left brain is analytical, linear, and processes information sequentially. Both hemispheres of the brain must be cultivated and balanced if one is to think and function properly. Balance must be maintained to have harmony throughout the body. The caduceus, the metaphysical paintings of The Christ, and the seemingly benign customs and rituals in our lives refer to the power that exists within us all.

The energy that flows into and though our body is regarded as a gift from the Creator. When this energy flowing through our bodies moves with ease, we experience health. If that energy flow is disrupted, we experience dis-ease, and become ill. Illness can affect us physically, mentally, socially, and spiritually. It is a state of being that must be understood if we are to attain high optimal performance from our bodies.

A mind which has been infused with creative energy is a powerful force. Its influence on the body, on other minds, and external circumstances is unlimited. Consciousness is one manifestation of the mind, and it represents a small fraction of the awesome power that is contained within. A mind and body that work in harmony with the spirit that directs them is capable of achieving infinite possibilities.

The ancient traditions of meditation and yoga were designed to teach people how to unite the energies within their mind and body so that they will come to know their higher spiritual selves. The acknowledgment of a consciousness that transcends physical consciousness opens a mind to limitless possibilities. These possibilities then allow you to exercise many more options to successfully overcome and avoid the difficulties in life.

References and Suggested Readings

Chopra, Deepak. *Ageless Body, Timeless Mind: The Quantum Alternative To Growing Old.* New York: Harmony Books, 1993.

Goleman, Daniel, and Gurin, Joel, eds. *Mind/Body Medicine: How to Use Your Mind for Better Health.* Yonkers, NY: Consumer Reports Books, 1993.

Moyers, Bill. *Healing And The Mind.* New York: Doubleday, 1993.

(Note: The Energy Spheres referenced in this Step may be purchased from the Institute of Karmic Guidance for $5.00 each, plus shipping and handling).

STEP 9.

Familiarize Yourself
with the Mysteries of Melanin

Imagine yourself among a group of enslaved Africans living on a plantation in Galveston, Texas on Monday, June 19, 1865. You are standing with your family, under the shade of a large tree when you are told by General Granger, of the Union Army, that the Civil War is over and all the slaves are now free. Try to visualize the feeling of joy and relief which sweeps over the crowd as they realize that their prayers have been answered.

But your excitement begins to diminish when you discover that the war had actually ended on April 9th of that year, and that your master withheld this news because he wanted to get his crops harvested before you left his plantation. As you struggle to begin life as a free human being, you slowly begin to realize that you have been technically freed by the Emancipation Proclamation two years, six months and eighteen days earlier. Words cannot describe your feelings of anger, frustration, and betrayal.

The memories of slavery haunt you day and night as you begin to realize that the promise of freedom, 40 acres and a mule, will never be realized. You understand, for the first time in your life, that you are truly on your own.

Fast forward into the future, exactly two months from today, you are watching CNN and the announcer tells you, "Scientists have confirmed that melanin is the key to health, longevity, and the optimal performance of human beings." As an African American, the news makes you ecstatic, and it also confirms long held beliefs which you have suppressed. Over the following weeks, as more news became available, you discover that knowledge of melanin was known years earlier and withheld by Europeans in order to give them an opportunity to manufacture artificial melanin for themselves.

Well, the future is now! Melanin has been proven to enhance human performance and Europeans are marketing artificial melanin for their special benefit. Do you now jump on the *Melanin Madness* bandwagon or will you take the time to familiarize

yourself with the mysteries of melanin? Be mindful of the fact
that a mystery is only a mystery as long as you're left in the dark.
With a little light-- knowledge and information--mysteries
disappear and are replaced with clarity and understanding.
European scientists have been researching melanin for over four
decades and have had annual meetings, behind closed doors, to
discuss and share their findings with their colleagues. There has
been very little public discussion of their research because melanin
is something Europeans possess in limited amounts and, therefore,
its significance was continually downplayed.

African and African American scholars and researchers have
studied melanin for over two decades.   In the 1970s, renowned
scientist, Dr. Cheikh Anta Diop, designed a "melanin dosage test"
that allowed him to illuminate and count the melaniated cells in
the skin tissue of royal Egyptian mummies and thus prove that
they were phenotypically "black" people.

In 1970, Dr. Frances Cress Welsing introduced *The Cress Theory
of Color Confrontation*, which linked racist, white supremacist
behavior with an absence of melanin. Since 1987, a collaboration of
melanin scholars and researchers have held conferences to
disseminate their findings to the African American community.

As can be expected, much of this research has been ignored by
academia and the mainstream media. African American scholars
have been labeled "racist," and their work "pseudo scientific," but
grassroots interest in the subject has steadily grown. Admittedly,
there have been some unsubstantiated claims concerning melanin
and its ability to enhance the performance of "people of color"--
this is always the case with any new discovery, but there is also a
wealth of valuable information that must not be dismissed.

For most Americans, interest in melanin grew tremendously in
1995 with the publication of a spate of books touting the benefits of
a naturally produced hormone called *melatonin*. Some of the titles
are: *The Melatonin Miracle; Melatonin: Your Body's Natural
Wonder Drug; Melatonin: The Anti-Aging Hormone;* and *Melatonin:
Nature's Sleeping Pill. Newsweek* devoted considerable space to
the subject of melatonin in the August 7 and November 6 issues
during 1995, as did a number of other publications and news sources
throughout the same year.

African Americans were advised not to follow the crowd in a
article entitled "Melanin Mania" written by T. Owens Moore, Ph.D.

This article appeared in the February 1996 issue of *Psyche Discourse*, the newsletter of the National Association of Black Psychologists. Dr. Moore is a psychologist who specializes in the relationship of the brain and behavior. He advised against the consumption of hormones developed in the laboratory that are unregulated by the Food and Drug Administration (FDA) and sold over the counter. He stated that there is no guarantee of melatonin purity and that the doses in many bottles are inaccurate. Dr. Moore concludes his article with the following words of caution:

All of the evidence . . . suggests that ethnic groups vary in their pineal-melatonin physiology. In other words, melatonin has a normal influence on circadian rhythms or the biological clock of African/Black people and it is not necessary to wind up the clock with more melatonin. What may be good for one ethnic group may not be good for another.

Through my organization, The Institute of Karmic Guidance, I have had the pleasure of hosting melanin conferences in Washington, D.C. in 1989 and 1994. My interaction with a host of African American melanin scholars has certainly increased my understanding of melanin, melatonin, and pineal gland research. I would recommend three publications for those interested in advancing their knowledge of melanin: *Melanin: The Chemical Key to Black Greatness*, by Carol Barnes, a polymer chemist; *The African Origin of Biological Psychiatry*, by psychiatrist Richard King, MD; and *The Science of Melanin: Dispelling the Myths*, by T. Owens Moore, Ph.D., psychology professor at Morehouse College.

Information gleaned from the pages of these works explains how melanin in the skin reduces the incidence of skin cancer and the role it also plays in eliminating free radicals which damage DNA and brain tissues and promotes cellular degradation (aging). Of particular interest are explanations as to why Africans, walk, talk, sing, dance, and worship the way we do. It's wonderful to gain insight and develop a deeper appreciation for being the unique creations of God that we are.

With this new found knowledge, I have been able to reevaluate particular experiences in my life with a greater sense of understanding. Both Mr. Barnes and Dr. Moore explain how melanin in the inner ear may enhance nerve impulses and "amplify the subsequent neurons in the auditory relay to the brain." This process synchronizes the movement of the body with the rhythm of the beat and helps Africans sing, snap their fingers, shake their heads, wiggle their hips, and move their feet, at the same time, without missing a beat. This "natural" motion is sometimes called "soul" and it is common among Africans, but a rare talent among "non-melaniated" people.

This relationship between melanin and musicians recalled to mind an experience I had at Howard University twenty-five years ago. In the summer of 1971, I enrolled in a class entitled "The History of Jazz," which was taught by Donald Byrd, the jazz trumpeter. Occasionally Mr. Byrd would invite other musicians to give the lecture. One evening, jazz guitarist George Benson met with our group and discussed his experiences in the music industry. He shared a story with the class which explained the concept of the *blue note*.

Most jazz aficionados are familiar with *Blue Note Records*, one of the most popular recording labels. R&B fans associate the word with the Philadelphia-based singing group, *Harold Melvin and the Blue Notes*. *Blue note* was a term popularized by African American musicians, but most people outside their circle were unfamiliar with its meaning.

Benson told the story of a discussion which took place between several African American jazz musicians during a gig in France. One of the musicians said he was approached by an aspiring French musician after the completion of a set. The Frenchman confided to the brother that he had listened to his performance over several evenings and took copious notes of the music that he heard.

The Frenchman stated that when he returned home to play the music he had jotted down on pieces of paper, the music sounded *strangely* different. The jazz musician let out a hardy laugh and told the Frenchman, "the problem, my brother, is that you can't hear the *blue note*." Benson went on to explain that, during the 1930s and 1940s, African American jazz musicians referred to the blue note as a range of musical notes that only African people were capable of hearing and feeling.

The various forms of musical expressions created by Africans in America (Spirituals, Blues, Jazz, Rhythm and Blues, Rock 'n Roll, Rap, and Hip Hop) have sustained the recording industry. The music of African Americans has given America a sense of soul music and dance that has influenced musical traditions throughout the world. This represents just one aspect of how melanin systems function in the bodies of African people. Similar achievements have been made by African American football, baseball, and basketball players. The very nature of professional sports was transformed when teams became integrated in the 1940s, 1950s, and 1960s. Historically, African Americans were excluded from sports because of the racist, white supremacist feelings exhibited by team owners, players, and fans alike. Jackie Robinson transformed the soul of baseball and opened the door for the giants who followed. Muhammad Ali brought a flair to boxing which had not existed since the days of Jack Johnson. His talent and outspokenness made him the most recognized human being on Earth. Throughout the entire history of the game of basketball, there has never been a player like Michael Jordan.

The historical record will show that African American athletes have added an element of excitement to their games which has revolutionized professional athletics throughout the world. However, one should not think that exceptional performances by Africans is limited to the stage and the sports arena. When given an opportunity to compete on a level-playing field, Africans generally excel. In light of this fact, one has to be truthful and admit that there is something unique about African people. Melanin can help explain that uniqueness.

Traditionally, Africans have been regarded by Europeans as very emotional and sentimental people. This truth was borne out in the response to the verdict of the 1995 murder trial of O.J. Simpson. Attorneys, politicians, and journalists nationwide lambasted attorney Johnny Cochran for "playing the race card" and "preying on the emotions of the blacks on the jury." The African American community was told that emotions are a poor substitute for intelligence and that feelings have no place in a cold and rational world. But feelings and emotions have helped Africans survive the hardships of enslavement, segregation, racism, and white supremacy that were created and sustained by people who perpetuated feelings and emotions of hatred, rage, and anger throughout the ages.

African Americans feel deeply because it is in our nature to feel. Our highly developed pineal glands secrete the hormones melatonin and serotonin that allow us to tap into a deep reservoir of ancestral memories. These memories hold the key to African consciousness. Dr. Richard King's work explores the depths of African biological psychiatry. He asserts that "the chemical key to life and the brain itself was . . . centered around black neuromelanin." King refers to the "locus coeruleus" (a concentration of heavily melaniated nerve cells within the brain) as the *Black Dot*, a doorway to the collective unconsciousness of humanity. It is this doorway that "the spirit" or "Holy Ghost" uses to enter the bodies of African people.

You can see this "spirit" manifest itself in many African American churches during the "call and response ritual." A special bond is established between the minister and the congregation when the worshipers are exalted by the words, rhythm, and movement of the preacher. The church resounds with "Amens" and shouts of "hallelujah" and the preacher is further invigorated by the exchange of energy. The tempo builds and builds until the entire church is filled with the spirit of the "Holy Ghost."

In some churches, people will get "happy" and begin "speaking in tongues" before passing out into the arms of a waiting attendant. This is a common occurrence in many "black" churches and is consistent with the spiritual traditions of Africans throughout the world. This special relationship that African people have with the spirit world (God, the ancestors, etc.) exists because of the presence of numerous melaniated centers in the body. It is thought that melanin acts as a conduit between the physical and metaphysical worlds.

Activating the "Black Dot consciousness" is an activity that many African Americans are already familiar with, they just never knew to refer to it as such. Do you recall hearing your elders discuss some of their unique methods for solving problems? When confronted with a decision of critical importance they would sometimes say, "Let me sleep on it for a while." After saying a few prayers and getting a good night's sleep they would arise in the morning and declare that "Aunt Mary" or "Cousin James," or some other ancestor, came to them in a dream and helped them decide what they should do.

This tradition of ancestral communication has existed in African societies for hundreds of years. It is the result of the secretion of the hormone melatonin into the brain during sleep.

This chemical produces an altered state of consciousness that allows the dreamer to communicate with ancestral spirits long gone. They ask questions and receive guidance. The secretion of the hormone serotonin, during daylight hours allows the dreamer to recall the dream and interpret its meaning.

Melatonin and serotonin serve as a natural call and response mechanism within the body. If they are understood as such and used properly, they can be of tremendous benefit, but if they are misunderstood or misused, one can easily be regarded as "crazy." Be mindful of the fact that emotion without historical memory is one of the clinical definitions of insanity. Africans are in possession of a wonderful physiological means to empower themselves by accessing their collective ancestral memory banks, but its proper use must be placed within a cultural context.

Africans must also be aware that some non-African religions consider this phenomena to be pagan and sacrilegious. Traditional Western medicine dismisses such activities as unscientific or primitive. In both instances, it is difficult for people, who lack certain abilities to condone what they do not understand and to appreciate what they fear.

Africans must study melanin and all related phenomena with the same intensity that we invest in our social, religious, athletic, and leisure activities. Our children should be exposed to this exciting field of study at an early age so that their young minds will be stimulated to consider scientific and technical careers that will allow them to explore new avenues of research. Melanin research and its many applications can have the same impact on society in the future as the computer has had within the past decade. The possibilities are limitless.

Since you have been advised to avoid artificially manufactured melatonin, it is appropriate that I provide you with ways to enhance melatonin production naturally:

1. Get plenty of rest and natural sunlight. It is always advisable to go to bed on the same day that you have awaken. For example, if you awake at 7 a.m., try to expose yourself to as much morning sunlight as possible. Sunlight stimulates the production of melatonin, which is secreted at night. You should also strive to go to bed before midnight of that same day and sleep in total darkness.

2. Eat foods which produce melatonin. Ripe bananas with brown spots and no trace of green, tomatoes, dark grapes, sweet corn, greens, and rice are all melatonin-producing foods. If you have difficulty sleeping, try eating any of these foods at least one hour before retiring and you should experience a night of restful sleep.

3. Consider adopting a vegetarian lifestyle. High-carbohydrate foods such as bread, rice, and pasta cause the body to produce more tryptophan, which is a natural precursor to melatonin. High-protein foods such as animal products restrict the amount of tryptophan in the blood system.

4. Consider natural vitamin and mineral supplements. Vitamins B3 and B6 help convert tryptophan to serotonin, a precursor of melatonin. It is advisable to take B6 earlier in the day and to consume B3 in the evening. Foods rich in B3 enhance the brain's output of melatonin, they include, turkey, tuna, barley, whole wheat, sunflower seeds, and dried apricots.

5. Maintain a low-calorie diet. Low-fat foods help increase the body's output of melatonin and are generally healthier for you.

6. Practice daily meditation. A 1995 study published by the University of Massachusetts Medical Center indicated that the pineal glands of women who meditated produced higher levels of melatonin than women who did not meditate.

7. **Limit your exposure to Electromagnetic fields (EMF's).** EMF's have been shown to affect the pineal gland, causing it to severely reduce the production of melatonin. EMF's are generated by computer monitors, copiers, electric blankets, dimmer switches, and poorly insulated electric wiring.

This partial listing of melatonin-inducing activities will help you increase your output of this very important hormone. When used in conjunction with the publications referenced in Step 9, you should develop a more thorough understanding of melanin and the role it plays in your overall development.

References and Suggested Readings

Barnes, Carol. *Melanin: The Chemical Key to Black Greatness.* Houston, TX: Black Greatness Series, 1988.

King, Richard M.D. *African Origin of Biological Psychiatry.* Germantown, TN: Seymour-Smith, Inc., P.O. Box 381063, 1990.

Moore, T. Owens. *The Science Of Melanin: Dispelling The Myths.* Silver Spring, MD: Venture Books/Beckham House Publishers, Inc, 1995.

(Note: Please call the Institute of Karmic Guidance for a listing of audio and video tapes of various topics pertaining to melanin).

Part Three

SPIRIT

The inhabitants of every society on earth have used mythology and symbolism in an attempt to understand the unexplainable events that have shaped their lives and influenced their destiny. Myths and symbols are the foundations on which ideals are fashioned and unite a people around common truths and understanding. Every religion or religious movement centers on the deification of a person and the historical record of that person's attempt to introduce specific metaphysical laws to followers.

There are certain physical and metaphysical constants within the universe which are experienced by all people. Their ethnic and cultural orientation determines how people respond to or interpret these universal constants. The many religions that have shaped the thinking of billions of people worldwide evolved out of this process. Each represents a methodology by which a follower can return to the Creator/God and achieve everlasting life.

The desire to understand God and find a suitable way to worship the Creator in order to secure the afterlife, has been the Achilles heal of many religious followers. Those who have sought power and control over others have used religion for political, social, economic, and nationalistic purposes. As a result, some religions have moved away from their original intent, which was the pursuit of spiritual enlightenment, and have used fear and violence as a means to amass wealth and power.

Spiritual enlightenment represents a way of knowing the Creator by understanding the manifestations of God that exist within the environment. All life is seen as embodying an aspect of the Creator. By knowing these aspects, one would come to know the Creator. This is the basic truth taught by many religious prophets who first sought spiritual enlightenment and then taught others how to attain it. Unfortunately, what has happened throughout the ages is that after the prophets died, they became the way, and their teachings were obscured by dogma.

Metaphorically, religion is to spirituality as a bucket is to a well. Religion is an instrument or vessel that allows a person to access the source of life, but it is not the source. Many messengers not only guided their followers to the wellspring of life, they also taught them that that source flows from within. Each person was deemed a vessel through which spirit flows. The degree of spirit that a person was able to access was determined by one's thoughts and deeds. When a person's thoughts were balanced and in harmony with their actions, blessings would flow in abundance, and they would achieve health, happiness, and prosperity.

Over the centuries, these teachings were obscured by self-serving individuals who would have you believe that you must go through them in order to access what is already yours. Be aware of these individuals Do not be afraid to seek the truth and ask questions of those who claim to hold the keys to your salvation. The nature of creation is such that you will always receive that which you truly seek and desire within your heart.

STEP 10.

Learn to Interpret Religious Imagery

Because I was born in America, I was raised in a Christian environment and, as a youth, attended church and Sunday school regularly. My grandmother, who was a deeply religious woman, devoted her life to God, the church, and her family. She was responsible for seeing to it that everyone in the household respected the teachings in the Bible.

As a young aspiring artist, I often drew pictures of scenes from my grandmother's Bible for various projects in Sunday school. When I began to discover my "blackness," I asked, "Why are there no pictures of black people in the Bible?" I never received a response that satisfied me. I was usually told that "God doesn't see color" and "we're all the same in The Lord's eyes." It became clear to me that if God didn't see color, those who created his image surely did.

As I grew older, I became aware that there were many religious denominations and numerous versions of the Bible. I realized that while many churches differed in their interpretation of God's word, they all seemed to agree on God's color--He was a white man, as was his son Jesus, all of the angels, and other biblical figures.

It wasn't until I saw the film, *Green Pastures*, that I became aware of the possibility that not only were there black people in the Bible, but that God Himself could be black. In my continuing efforts to find a place for African people in world history, I have come to discover that the universal image of a "white" God has been in existence for less than seventeen hundred years. Biblical research shows that the earliest spiritual/theological concepts took shape in the Nile Valley over six thousand years ago.

Africans, the first humans and the first people to develop culture, civilization, and religion, believed that every aspect of their lives was influenced by a powerful creative spirit that we now call *God*. This spirit had the ability to manifest itself in various ways and *nature* was its divine handiwork. Every aspect of nature was a reflection of an aspect of the Creator, and by studying these aspects, it was possible to know oneself and understand the Creator.

Africans in the Nile Valley developed spiritual systems that acknowledged the existence of *one* divine Creator. They also had the intelligence to realize that this one Creative source was capable of manifesting itself in many ways. Over six thousand years ago, the priests of Kemet identified thirty-six manifestations of the Creator, which were known collectively as the *Netecherw* and individually as *Netcher*. A Netcher represents one principle or aspect of the divine Creator, and Netecherw were depicted as complementary pairs of eighteen males and females.

Throughout Kemetic history, philosophy, and symbolic thought, we see frequent references to one of the most important principles of nature--balance and harmony of the masculine and feminine principles of the Creator. The harmonic expression of these principles was necessary for the creation, maintenance, balance, and harmonious operation of the universe. It is from the word "Netcher" that modern man has derived the word *nature*. So when modern man speaks of *Mother Nature*, he is talking about the feminine aspect of the Creator. If there is a feminine aspect of the Creator, there also has to be a masculine aspect of the Netecherw, or *Father Nature*.

There was a Netcher, called *Shu*, who was associated with air, and his female counterpart was *Teftnut*, the Netcher associated with wind. The sky was represented by the Netcher *Nut* and her male counterpart was Geb, the *Netcher* who personified the earth or soil. Among the elements of nature, the sun was considered to be one of the most powerful visible expressions of the Creator. It was symbolized by several Netecherw as it moved across Nut--the sky. *Heru* was the morning sun, *Re* represented the midday sun, and *Amen* was the evening sun. These aspects of the sun later personified the three stages of life that every person would experience: infancy, adulthood, and eldership.

All of the aspects of the Netcherw were organized by and functioned under the auspices of *Maat*. Maat was a female Netcher who represented truth, justice, propriety, harmony, balance reciprocity, and order. Maat was the balance upon which each soul was to be weighed on the day of judgment. After 6,234 years, this spiritual system still exists, in varying degrees, as the cornerstone of the religions of Judaism, Christianity, and Islam.

One of the most significant aspects of African spiritual traditions can be found in the story of the African Holy Trinity of Ausar, Aset, and Heru, which was discussed briefly in Step 5. It is critically important to understand that Ausar was the first person in recorded history who was said to have been murdered and later resurrected from his grave as a God. Aset was the first virgin on record to become spiritually impregnated and give birth to the son of God on December 25. All of these images and concepts were carved on the walls of temples and painted on papyri in Kemet thousands of years ago, and they can still be seen today.

I have shown these images to the hundreds of people who have traveled to Egypt with me on my annual study tours. Their significance is often overwhelming. There have been a number of clergy on these tours, some of whom have willingly shared this information with their congregations on their return to the United States. Others have confided to me that they would be out of a job if they discussed what they saw with their congregations. While I appreciated their candor, I was sorely disappointed in their unwillingness to teach the truth.

Most people are unaware of the extent to which African spiritual and religious concepts were Europeanized and presented to the world as original religious constructs. The parallels between the two teachings are obvious when they are compared. The challenging part is learning to accept the fact that what has been presented as an original truth, existed thousands of years earlier in a different image and form. It doesn't minimize the message, it only causes one to look at the messenger somewhat differently.

The truth of the matter is that the religious teachings practiced in most churches today stem from decisions made by European males less than two thousand years ago. They have been sanitized, canonized, and passed down from generation to generation as unquestionable truths. The celebration of Christmas on December 25, for example, has nothing to do with the birth of Jesus because no one knows when Jesus was born. Christian bishops in the fourth century adopted December 25 because it was the most universally celebrated day for the birth of numerous Gods throughout the world. There were over a dozen religious figures who were said to have been born of December 25, and they all lived before the birth of Jesus.

The average person knows little about the history of religion other than what they have been told by their pastor or what they have read in one book, the Bible. Our perceptions of God and related religious imagery were created for us by others. In many instances, religion has been used by one group to dehumanize people who held beliefs different than theirs. Religion has historically been used to empower one group of people, while rendering another group spiritually ravished. Central to the control of a people is the control of their concept and image of God and the desecration of their religious iconography. A study of the religious wars fought over the ages validates this fact.

During the Crusades, historic battles between Christian and Muslims were fought over control of Jerusalem. Unspeakable atrocities were committed by both parties during the course of a struggle that lasted almost 200 years. While the proposed intent of the war was to recapture the holy city seized by the Muslims, some Europeans used the war as a means to increase their power, territory, and riches.

Thousands of men, women, and children, on both sides of the conflict, were raped, murdered, and enslaved. The objective of both opposing forces was the destruction and humiliation of their opponents. In one instance, the bakers in a southern European town made their bread in the shape of a crescent moon (a symbol of the Islamic faith). Each morning residents were encourged to eat "croissants" as a symbol of their desire to devour the Muslim army.

The act of defiling religious symbols has continued throughout modern times. When the Iranian revolutionaries seized the U.S. Embassy in Teheran and took American employees hostage, anti-Islamic sentiments was rampant throughout the nation. The popularity of the croissant reached an all time high as Americans directed their hatred toward Iraq and other Islamic terrorists.

While one segment of American society may be unconsciously denigrating a religious symbol, another is struggling to reclaim a religious icon--the Black Christ. The current movement to portray Jesus as a black man has grown from the fact that many African American Christians have become increasingly aware of the falsification of religious iconography by Europeans. As early as 1829, Robert Young, an African American nationalist, taught his followers that Jesus was of African descent. Henry McNeal Turner echoed similar sentiments in 1894, and a host of other African Americans followed suit throughout the twentieth century.

In 1992, the African American Catholic Congregation launched its *Black Christ/Black Church Project* in an effort to correct historical, theological, and biblical distortions about the true identity of Jesus. In 1993, a number of African American theologians contributed to the creation of the *Original African Heritage Study Bible*; a Bible that corrects many of the errors of earlier editions and clearly defines and depicts the presence of African people throughout the Bible.

In the April 1995 edition of *Emerge* Magazine, the cover story was "Is Jesus Black?" The article contained interviews with several African American ministers and religious scholars who discussed the importance of identifying and reclaiming the African presence in the Bible. In addition to this movement to revise the Bible, there must also be an examination of why biblical images were changed and the effect those changes have had on the psyche of African people.

The renowned African American psychologist, Dr. Na'im Akbar addressed the issue of "Racial Religious Imagery" in his publication *Breaking the Chains of Psychological Slavery*:

> . . . if you have internalized the view of the deity as being in the flesh, having a nationality and physical differences different from yourself, then you automatically assume that your are inferior in your characteristics. The sense of inferiority is not in the form of 'natural humility'. . . but you begin to believe you have less human potential than one who looks like the image.

The Association of Black Psychologists took a professional stand on this matter and approved a resolution at their 1980 annual meeting:

> . . . the display of the Divine in images of Caucasian flesh constitutes an oppressive instrument destructive to the self-esteem of Black people throughout the world and is directly destructive to the psychological well-being of Black children.

The resolution also stated that Caucasian images of the Creator and other Divine figures advocated white supremacy while simultaneously implying "Black inferiority." The Association provided copies of their resolution to religious and civil rights organizations throughout America, in an effort to establish "an educational dialogue for change."

The rise of the Black Consciousness Movement in the 1960s and the current movement towards African Centeredness have prompted millions of African Americans to reevaluate the traditional European presentation of world history and religious history. African history and culture are now looked on more favorably by Africans in America, and we now have a greater desire to reclaim our lost history. Because a majority of the events in the Bible took place in Africa, it is only natural that we seek to reclaim that aspect of our history too.

While African Christians in America are slowly returning to the sources of biblical history, many Africans on the continent continue to be bombarded with a racist and outdated, hard-line version of Christianity. In Ghana, for example, there are dozens of billboards throughout the countryside that portray Jesus as a blue-eyed, blond European. The passage on one billboard stated: *"Right hand implies power, therefore, sitting on the right hand of God means reigning in the capacity of God, all creation is under him. John 8:16, 23 and 42."*

Right hand implies power. Therefore sitting on the right hand of God means reigning in the capacity of God. All creation is under him.
John 8:16, 23, 42

These billboards are sponsored by the West African Evangelical Society, which is largely financed by European American Christians. Their presence raises two particularly disturbing issues. The first involves the inaccurate portrayal of the image of Jesus at a time when most theologians agree that Jesus was not European. Ghana was the first African nation to liberate itself from European colonialism and the proliferation of European images of Jesus must be interpreted as an attempt to recolonize the minds and spirits of the Ghanaian people. One of the most frequently used tactics of colonial invaders was the dispatching of *missionaries* to soften the hearts and minds of a people and then the sending of *mercenaries* to conquer their land.

The second concern about the billboard has to do with the passage, *"Right hand implies power . . ."* which does not exist in John 8:16, 23 or 42. I consulted several ministers and they were unaware of the existence of this passage in any version of the Bible. They openly expressed contempt for the manner in which the Ghanaians were being duped by unscrupulous opportunists. I also had conversations with a number of Ghanaian Christians who were unaware of the inaccuracy of the image and text on the billboards. They had mistakenly assumed that the information was valid because it was sanctioned by European American missionaries.

Somewhere in the annals of European literature someone once wrote that "ignorance is bliss;" but in the ancient record of African philosophy is the belief that "ignorance is sinful." Most of us have been conditioned to live our lives in a sinful state of blissful ignorance while thinking we were actually being saved. If we equated ignorance with sinfulness we would be more inclined to conduct independent research into the origins of our current beliefs and practices. We would then become aware of many startling revelations.

We would know that the early Greek and Roman Christians portrayed Jesus as a person of African ancestry. Justinian I, the Eastern Roman emperor who ruled from 527 to 565 A.C.E., commissioned coins to be minted with the face of an African Jesus on one side and his own distinctively European face on the other. Many Europeans of this era revered Africans and openly worshipped the "Black Madonna and Child" in shrines throughout Europe. As Europeans became more nationalistic, they developed a psychological need to create God in their own image, and the complexion of their religious icons changed from black to white. When Europeans began to colonize the world and enslave people of color, they imposed this new image of God on those they conquered. Michelangelo's painting of Adam and Eve in the Sistine. Chapel in Rome, Italy is still accepted by people throughout the world as the legitimate likeness of the first couple. No one suspected that Michelangelo's aunt and uncle were the models for the painting in 1508. Most of us have seen the image of Jesus the Christ and his disciples as portrayed by Leonardo da Vinci in his painting "The Last Supper." We have been captivated by the beauty of this fifteenth century masterpiece, but few of us know that da Vinci hired a model to pose as Jesus, and 12 convicts to pose as his disciples. In reality, the image that we have held in such high esteem is unworthy of the admiration it has been given. It is a technically flawless painting but a terribly deceptive religious icon.

Throughout most of our lives, we have been conditioned to live with distortions that were fabricated to substantiate the superiority of others. When these concerns are raised, there are those within the African family who will respond by saying that *"color is not important,"* or that *"it doesn't matter if Jesus is Black, White or Brown."* The flaw in that logic is, if it did not matter hundreds of years ago, then the images would never have been altered. If it does not matter today, then Europeans should have no objection to correcting the false images and worshipping a politically and spiritually correct image of Jesus. But I am certain this will never happen in our lifetime.

I am particularly concerned about the latent effect these images have had on African people over many generations. This concern intensified in 1993 when I was giving a presentation at a U.S. Air Force Base in Misawa, Japan during Black History Month. Prior to my introduction, the base chaplain, who was an African American, gave the invocation which he ended with the traditional closing, "Amen."

During the course of my presentation, I made reference to the invocation and asked for a show of hands of those who were aware that the word "Amen" is actually the name of an African Netcher. Only four or five of the 300 people in attendance raised their hands. I informed the others that the word *Amon* or *Amen* references "the hidden or the unseen presence of God" and represented the ever-present power of God/the sun which exists even after the sun/God disappears from view.

The following Sunday, a number of persons who attended my lecture asked the pastor whether my comments regarding the African origin of the word *Amen* were accurate. The pastor verified the accuracy of my remarks. Some members responded by saying that if the word *Amen* really did refer to an African God, they would never use it again. I was shocked when I was told of their decision, but the exchange confirmed the fact that even when given an opportunity to see themselves in the image of the Creator, mis-educated Negroes will reject the opportunity every single time.

This incident helped to convince me of the grave psychological and spiritual harm African people have suffered at the hands of their oppressors. It leads me to conclude that if Jesus the Christ did return to Earth as a black man, He would probably be rebuked by blacks and whites alike.

Ever-increasing numbers of African American Christians are involved in a national movement to reclaim the African identity of biblical personalities. If the Black Christ movement is justified, then what are the broader implications of the deceptive use of religious imagery by Europeans over the past 500 years? Consider the significance of the following questions. Ponder them earnestly and, if you are willing, pose these questions to your family members and friends, and engage them in a meaningful dialogue.

Before answering the following five questions, it is advisable to read the introduction and preface of the *Original African Heritage Study Bible*. It provides useful background information. I would also encourage you to apply the critical thinking skills discussed in Step 5. Do not settle for literal interpretations of these questions. Base your conclusions on what you know to be verifiable facts.

1. If Adam and Eve, Noah, Moses, and Jesus the Christ were all of African ancestry, then what affect does this knowledge have on you today?

2. Was there a relationship between the sanctioning by the Roman Catholic Church of the enslavement of Africans in 1442, and the continued use of biblical scripture to justify the enslavement of Africans in America?

3. Why do you believe the Southern Baptist Convention waited until June 1995 to publicly denounce the acts of racism that they had condoned throughout their first 150 years of existence?

4. If the color of Jesus' skin is not a relevant issue, then why do you think he was portrayed as European for over 500 years?

5. Do you believe that most Americans are willing to embrace an African image of Christ?

References and Suggested Readings

ben-Jochannan, Yosef. *African Origins of the Major Western Religions.* Baltimore, MD: Black Classic Press, 1991.

Blyden, Edward W. *Christianity, Islam and the Negro Race.* Baltimore, MD: Black Classic Press, 1994.

Emerge Magazine, *Is Jesus Black?*, April 1995, (Cover Story).

Felder, Cain Hope. *Troubling Biblical Waters: Race, Class and Family,* Maryknoll, NY: Orbis Books, 1989.

Jones, Terry & Ereira, Alan. *Crusades.* New York: Facts on File, 1995.

The Original African Heritage Study Bible, King James Version. Nashville, TN: James C. Winston Publishing Co., 1993.

Walker, Wyatt Tee. *Afrocentrism & Christian Faith.* New York: Martin Luther King Fellows Press, 1993.

(Note: Of additional interest is a short story, *The Boy Who Painted Christ Black,* written by Dr. John Henrik Clarke. This story was made into a film and incorporated in a trilogy of short stories which aired on HBO in February 1996. It is an engaging story which depicts the struggles of southern blacks in a segregated school, and a child who enters a painting of Christ in an art contest. *Opportunity Magazine,* Urban League, 1940).

Remember always these Selections From The Husia, The Sacred Wisdom of Ancient Kemet:

Be skilled in speech so that you will succeed. The tongue of a man is his sword and effective speech is stronger than all fighting. None can overcome the skillful. A wise person is a school for the nobles and those who are aware of his knowledge do not attack him. No evil takes place when he is near. Truth comes to him in its essential form, shaped in the sayings of the ancestors.

Follow in the footsteps of your ancestors, for the mind is trained through knowledge. Behold, their words endure in books. Open and read them and follow their wise counsel.

The Book of Kheti

*   *   *   *   *   *   *

Pour libation for your father and mother who rest in the valley of the dead. God will witness your action and accept it. Do not forget to do this even when you are away from home. For as you do for your parents, your children will do for you also.

The Book of Ani

STEP 11.

Learn to Honor the Memory of Your Ancestors

The United States comprises many groups of immigrants who, in their quest to become Americans, have willingly retained their language, customs, and the traditions of their ancestors. The groups who have faired well, overcoming racial, economic, and social barriers are those who have, unashamedly, retained linguistic, cultural, and ancestral ties with their motherland.

As I travel throughout the country, I discover, in practically every city, a Chinatown, a Greektown, Irish, Italian, and Polish cultural centers and churches that cater to the needs of specific ethnic communities. Many of these communities have elementary schools, high schools, colleges, and universities that were created specifically to socialize students and instill within them the legacy of their ancestors.

Dr. Asa G. Hilliard, III, an educational psychologist and historian, is the author of *The Maroon Within Us*, a selection of essays on "African American community socialization." In this work, Dr. Hilliard discusses a number of historical and social issues of critical importance to the African American community. Hilliard reminds us that "the survival of a group's identity is directly proportional to the degree to which it can replenish its identity through education, ritual, and role taking."

In numerous lectures throughout the country, Dr. Hilliard has brought to the attention of the community a somewhat obscure work entitled *Tribes*, which was written by Joel Kotkin. In *Tribes*, Kotkin, a business trends analyst for Fox Television, identifies five tribes/ethnic groups who are poised to triumph in the international arenas of business, technology, and communications in the twenty-first century: the British, Jews, Japanese, Chinese, and Indians.

Kotkin contends that these ethnic groups will thrive because they use "race, religion, and identity to determine success in the new global economy." All of these groups have thrived in the United States for these very same reasons. They *know who they are*, they *retain their culture*, and they have a *cultural relationship to their God*.

When the British came to America, they brought their culture with them and they named the states of New York, New Hampshire, and New Jersey after locations reminiscent of their homeland. Over time the eastern seaboard has come to be known as "New England," and the language of their ancestors is now the "unofficial" language of the land. The laws of England have formed the backbone of American law, and the Protestant religion can also be considered the dominate religion in a nation still governed largely by white Anglo-Saxon Protestants.

Even the European Jew, who is considered non-white by European standards, has also found a comfortable niche in American society. They have stridently retained their language, culture, and religion and have established an economic, educational, and political powerbase within American society. Currently, the state of Israel receives more U.S. financial support than all of the nations in Africa. Even though Jews number only 6 million, they wield considerable power and influence.

In April 1993, members of the Jewish American community celebrated the opening of The United States Holocaust Museum in Washington, D.C. The Jewish community contributed $150 million to construct this museum which memorializes Jewish victims of the Nazi death camps during the Second World War in Europe. The building was designed by a Jewish architect who incorporated into its structure numerous elements symbolic of Jewish struggle and resistance. As of January 1, 1994, U.S. tax dollars are now being spent to maintain the museum.

The steps taken by Jewish Americans to honor the memory of their ancestors and preserve their history are noteworthy and should be of particular interest to African Americans. We must ask ourselves, where is the national memorial honoring the memory of the Africans who died during the European Slave Trade? Where is the national museum honoring the enslaved Africans whose labor made it possible for Americans to enjoy the highest standard of living in the world?

When these questions are asked, the typical response of "misguided Negroes" is that slavery is something that happened in the past, and we must learn to forgive and forget, and leave the past behind. One of the reasons why Africans are still struggling for basic freedoms in this country is because we have forgotten how we came to America, and we have forgiven those who brought us here. It makes no sense for Africans to believe that we continue to pay a price for the sins of Adam and Eve, who lived over 4,000 years ago, and yet we are unaffected by the actions of slave traders who lived less than 150 years ago.

African Americans lack a national museum simply because we do not fully understand the importance of studying and preserving our history. We also do not fully understand the significance of pooling our resources and establishing institutions in memory of our ancestors. Money is not an issue because the African American community spends over $400 billion annually. We are not poor people; we just exercise poor judgment.

There are many unfortunate Negroes in this country who are ashamed of their African heritage. They will proudly proclaim that they are part Indian, or Italian, or French, or Irish, or any other ethnic group while simultaneously denying the African face which stares back at them in the mirror. They lament daily over the condition of their African hair, the only part of their anatomy that willingly proclaims its African roots.

Third generation Italians, who have never been to Italy, preserve their culture by celebrating Columbus Day. Third or fourth generation Irish who have lived in America all of their lives still revere Irish history and celebrate St. Patrick's Day. Mexican Americans living in the United States continue to celebrate Cinco de Mayo, because they respect the cultural accomplishments of their ancestors.

Many African Americans see nothing wrong with celebrating the culture of others, but are too embarrassed to celebrate their own. On a typical St. Patrick's Day you will probably find as many African Americans wearing green as you would Irish Americans. Yet these same people would not be caught dead wearing a kufi or Kente cloth, or celebrating Kwanzaa. Admittedly, the clothing people wear is certainly no guarantee of their allegiance to a particular culture, but it is a tangible indication of their consciousness.

African Americans are the only group who came to America with an invitation and with a guarantee of full employment-- whether we wanted it or not! We were not allowed to bring our history, our culture, or our own ways of relating to the Creator. After 350 years, we are still dependent on our former slave masters to employ us, educate us, protect us, and provide for our overall well-being.

We don't invest in our native land, and we have no national museum to honor the tens of millions of Africans who died in enslavement in the United States. We have been trained to forget our ancestors. In the eyes of the world, any group that does not honor the memory of their ancestors is unworthy of respect.

Africans in America have been programmed to forget 400 years of rapes, lynchings, beatings, and murders. While it is not practical that we seek "an eye for an eye," it is impractical for us to turn a blind eye to these atrocities. Africans in America must never forget the most horrific event which humanity has ever witnesses . . . the *Maafa*, a Kiswahili word which means "Great Disaster." Maafa refers to the sufferings of over 100 million African people who were enslaved and murdered since 1442, and the beginning of the European Slave Trade of African people. The Maafa continues today and many African Americans are still dealing with the post traumatic effects of slavery.

African Americans have been taught to feel ashamed of slavery. It's as if it were our own fault; as if our ancestors begged the Europeans to take them from their homelands in chains and rape their mothers, daughters, and sons. Dr. Martin Luther King, Jr. addressed this issue and put it in its proper perspective when he stated: "I for one am not ashamed of this past. My shame is for those who became so inhuman that they would inflict this torture upon us."

If we truly understood the extent of the atrocities perpetrated against African people, we would never feel shame. Instead, we would feel duty bound to honor the memory of the men, women, and children who suffered at the hands of people who demonstrated little remorse for their actions. If you listen . . . you can hear the souls of the dead crying. They are crying for justice, and they are crying to remind you and me that what happened in the past can happen in the future.

It is difficult to truly comprehend the ramifications of the Maafa, but let us take a moment and look at some aspects of this great disaster. The term *Maafa* was introduced to the African community by Dr. Dona Richards in her publication *Let The Circle Be Unbroken*. Dr. Richards, who has now changed her name to Marimba Ani, is a social scientist and professor of Black Studies at

Hunter College, City University of New York. In *Let The Circle Be Unbroken*, she wrote about the impact of the Maafa on the African family in America:

> The system and circumstances of slavery in New Europe [America] sought to destroy African value, African self-image and self-concept. The African universe was disrupted. It became dysfunctional as the sense of order that it offered dissolved. For the overwhelming majority of those brought to North America and their direct descendants, the benefits of African culture were stripped away—not one by one—but brutally, in one sudden and total act. Family, language, kinship patterns, food, dress and formalized religion were gone. What replaced them was the order of slavery. The objective of the new order was to demonstrate our lack of value. It turned our humanity into weakness. To be European was to have value, to be African was to be without personal worth . . . the slave order created and depended on a constant state of terror. As long as you denied your Africaness, your humanness, and pretended that you didn't mind watching others suffer around you, you were relatively safe. For fear [was] the great immobilizer.

Africans in America should never be ashamed of the indignities that our ancestors were forced to endure during enslavement. We should never refer to them as *slaves*, for they were human beings who were *enslaved* by others of a subhuman nature. We must not be afraid to confront this dreadful period of our history, for there are valuable lessons we can learn from this past that will allow us to move forward with courage and direction.

There are other meaningful publications that shed light on the horrors of enslavement. A document entitled "Let's Make A Slave" was brought to the public's attention by attorney Robert L. Brock. He discovered it while researching documents in the basement of a courthouse in the South. "Let's Make A Slave" is a study of the physical and psychological process called "seasoning" which was designed to break the spirit of newly arrived Africans and prepare them for a lifetime of servitude.

[The methods used to "make a slave" were gruesome and indicative of the vicious nature of the enslavement process. [In one particular example, citing the "Cardinal principles for making a Negro," the author states:

WOW! !

> Take the meanest and most restless nigger, strip him of his clothes in front of the . . . [slaves], tar and feather him, tie each leg to a different horse faced in opposite directions, set him afire and beat both horses to pull him apart in front of the remaining nigger[s]. The next step is to take a bull whip and beat the remaining nigger to the point of death in front of the female and infant. Don't kill him but put the fear of God in him, for he can be useful for future breeding.

The writers of this document described the psychological impact this murder and beating would have on the enslaved female and infant:

> In her natural uncivilized state she would have a strong dependency on the uncivilized nigger male, and she would have a limited protective tendency toward her independent male offspring and would raise the female offspring to be dependent like her. Nature had provided for this type of balance. We reversed nature by burning and pulling one uncivilized nigger apart and bullwhipping the other to the point of death—all in her presence. [By her being left alone, unprotected, with the male image destroyed, the ordeal caused her to move from her psychological dependent state to a frozen independent state. | In this frozen psychological state of independence, she will raise her male and female offspring in reversed roles. For fear of the young male's life, she will psychologically train him to be mentally weak and dependent but physically strong. Because she has become psychologically independent, she will train her female offspring to be psychologically independent. . . . You've got the nigger woman out front and the nigger man behind and scared. This is a perfect situation for sound sleep and good economics.

The psychological effects of the Maafa were designed to endure for hundreds of years. In 1712, plantation owners from the state of Virginia invited a European plantation owner from Barbados, named William Lynch, to share with them his techniques for controlling enslaved Africans. Mr. Lynch delivered the following remarks on the banks of the James River in Virginia:

> . . . I have here a fool proof method for controlling your Black Slaves. I guarantee everyone of you that if installed correctly, it will control your slaves for at least 300 years. My Method is simple, any member of your family or any overseer can use it. . . . I have outlined a number of differences among the slaves and I take these differences and make them bigger. I use fear, distrust, and envy for control purposes. . . . The Black slave, after receiving this indoctrination will carry on and will become self refueling and self generating for hundreds of years, maybe thousands. Don't forget, you must pitch the old Black male versus the young Black male. The young Black male against the old Black male. You must use the dark skin slaves against the light skin slaves and the light skin slaves against the dark skin slaves. You must use the female against the male and the male against the female. You must also have your white servants and overseers distrust all Blacks. It is necessary that your slaves trust and depend on us. They must love, respect and trust only us. . . . Gentlemen, these kits are your keys to control. Use them. /Have your wives and children use them. Never miss an opportunity. If used intensely for one year, the slaves themselves will remain perpetually distrustful. /

Many of the "methods" devised by William Lynch continue to influence the behavior of millions of Africans throughout the urban plantations of America. We were programmed to be distrustful of one another in the past and we continue to be distrustful of each other today. Many of us still believe that light-skin blacks are smarter, more intelligent, and prettier than dark-skin blacks. We denigrate ourselves by saying that "light skin" is "fair skin" and that "straight hair" is "good hair." We continue to use the language of brainwashed people to debase ourselves, while believing that such language does no harm to ourselves or our children.

|"Brainwashed" is an appropriate adjective to describe the process of making a slave.|The desire to destroy the consciousness of African people is apparent when you examine the comments made by Henry Berry, a delegate of the Virginia House of Representatives in 1832. Mr. Berry addressed his associates, on the floor of the Virginia House of Representatives:

> We have as far as possible, closed every avenue by which light may enter the slaves' mind. . . . [I]f we could extinguish the capacity to see the light, our work would be complete, they would then be on a level with the beast of the field and we should be safe.

Central to the process of enslaving Africans was the reconfiguration of their minds and the creation of a Negro consciousness. Our ancestors were brutally disconnected from their past, forbidden from reclaiming and celebrating it, and, therefore, unable to adequately provide for the well-being of future generations. We must never forget that the Constitution of the United States denied Africans their human and civil rights. African family life was shattered, ancestral and spiritual practices were denied, and it was illegal for Africans to read or write.

These conditions existed for approximately twelve generations and account for the economic, educational, and social disparities that now exist between African and Europeans in America. Within the European American community, the wealth gained from the labor of Africans was passed on from one generation to the next. It was used to build industries, towns, cities, states, and the wealth of a nation. The creators of newly formed empires were continually honored by their descendants who established foundations, libraries, and awards in their memory.

Today, those ancestors are honored by days which celebrate their legacy and birth. Thanksgiving was established to honor the memory of the earliest settlers in America. The birthdays of George Washington, Abraham Lincoln, or Robert E. Lee are commemorated to honor the spirits of these men. Memorial Day, Labor Day, and Veterans' Day were established so that the people would long remember those who gave their lives defending and building this nation.

It makes perfect sense to honor the memory of one's ancestors because they are a continual source of strength and inspiration. Africans have long known this to be a fact, and in their homeland, they developed rituals which, I believe, helped them survive the Maafa. There is no group of people on earth who have suffered as long and as hard as Africans. The mere fact that we are alive today, many of us with our minds and souls intact, is a testament to the spirit that dwells within us. This spirit must be honored and nurtured if we are to create a meaningful existence for the souls we will bring into the world.

There is an African proverb which says, "If you speak the name of the dead, they will never die." Western science has confirmed the fact that matter nor energy can be created or destroyed. They simply change form. Africans believed that when a person becomes an ancestor, their spirit remains connected to the collective consciousness of their people. The act of remembering the ancestors, through libation and ritual, links them to the living. As spirit, the ancestors are linked to the Creator, serve as our intermediaries, and are eventually reborn into the community. Thus, the deceased, the living, and the yet unborn are all connected in a cultural and cosmic circle which binds the past, present, and future.

Our genes and the melanin in our bodies are vital components in this cycle. The genetic material passed on from generation to generation is our pipeline to our ancestors. Look at yourself. Are you told you have your father's eyes, your mother's complexion, your grandmother's hands, your great-grandfather's disposition? You are a manifestation of all of the ancestors who have come before you. The melaniated centers within your body, particularly your pineal gland, allow you to access your ancestral superhighway.

This ancestral structure is similar, in essence, to the Internet. There exists, within the spiritual universe, a network of unlimited possibilities. In order to log on to your ancestral data base, you must have an access code, the proper equipment, and you must possess some idea of where you want to go. A melaniated body is optimally equipped and comes with scores of melaniated microprocessors and the fastest modem known to man—the pineal gland. ⎰Rituals are your access code and your direction is provided by your culture.⎱ *This Part*

Dr. Theophile Obenga, a colleague of the late, Dr. Cheikh Anta Diop, addressed an informal gathering several years ago and discussed the significance of ancestral communion. He told us that, "We are the ancestors. They live in us and operate through us." I am convinced that by reclaiming the knowledge of our past, we learn the rituals necessary to effectively honor and commune with our ancestors. By communing with our ancestors, we are able to access empowering levels of knowledge which will allow us to transform our consciousness, and create, through our thoughts and actions, a world worthy of passing on to our children.

This is what sets our culture apart; makes us special!!

Whenever we embark on a new journey or undertaking, it is important to have a clear vision of where we are going and the best way to get there. Listed below are two publications I would strongly urge you to read to gain a deeper understanding of African spirituality, ancestral communion, and rituals:

Let The Circle Be Unbroken: The Implications of African Spirituality in the Diaspora by Dr. Dona Marimba Richards. This is a small book of sixty pages that contains clear and concise information about the spiritual dimensions of African culture. It is an invaluable treasure which covers a broad range of topics and provides meaningful insights into numerous aspects of African and African American life.

The second publication is, *The African Personality in America: An African-Centered Framework* by Kobi Kambon. Dr. Kambon is a professor of psychology and chair of the Psychology Department at Florida A & M University. He is an expert in the areas of personality and social psychology. His book explores a number of topics pertaining to the nature of the "African Personality" as well as its structure and development. Of particular importance is Chapter 8, "Reclaiming Our Africanity: Applications of African Self-Consciousness Theory." Kambon provides an explanation of the meaning and purpose of libations and offers a detailed example. He also provides a similar explanation of ancestor communion and offers a ritual designed to help people reclaim their African identity.

Also included in Chapter 8 is an Africancentric Calendar which lists numerous dates of cultural significance, an African Personality glossary, and extensive references. *African Personality in America* is a perfect companion to *Let The Circle Be Unbroken* and Dr. Kambon references Dr. Richards frequently throughout his work.

In addition to the recommended readings, I would also suggest that you secure the following materials for your personal library.

(1)   The film *Sankofa* is a must-see for every person of African descent. It is a powerful story of the trials and tribulations of a group of enslaved Africans on a plantation in the Caribbean. It vividly portrays the beauty and power of African ancestral spirits. *Sankofa* is now available on videotape and may be ordered directly from the distributor by calling 202-289-6677 or 1-800-524-3895.

(2)   *The Middle Passage: White Ships/Black Cargo*, is a masterfully illustrated book by award winning artist, Tom Feelings. It is a moving and powerful visual narrative of the capture of Africans and the dreaded middle passage.

(3)   *Africa On My Mind: Reflections of My Second Trip* is the second book that I have co-authored with my daughter, Atlantis. It deals with her journey to West Africa and visits to numerous cities, villages and slave dungeons in four nations. *Africa On My Mind* broadens ones understand of African and African American history and is an excellent primer for youth and adults.

(4)   *Bullwhip Days-The Slaves Remember: An Oral History* is a collection of interviews with formerly enslaved African Americans. It tells their stories of the harsh realities of enslavement and provides "sobering insight into the roots of racism in today's society."

(5)   *Of Water and the Spirit: Ritual, Magic, and Initiation in the Life of an African Shaman* is a magical autobiography of Malidoma Some' and his early years in Burkina Faso, West Africa. It is a captivating story of Malidona's childhood, his abduction by French priests, and his struggle to return to his village. The highlight of this book is Maladoma's riveting description of the ritual he was required to go through prior to his return to his village.

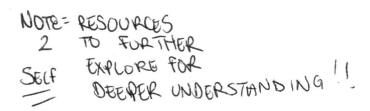

NOTE = RESOURCES
2   TO FURTHER
SELF   EXPLORE FOR
         DEEPER UNDERSTANDING !!

References and Suggested Readings

Browder, Atlantis Tye & Anthony T. *Africa On My Mind: Reflections Of My Second Trip*. Washington, D.C.: The Institute of Karmic Guidance, 1995.

Feelings, Tom. *The Middle Passage: White Ships/Black Cargo*. New York: Dial Books, 1995.

Kambon, Kobi Kazembe Kalongi. *The African Personality in America: An African-Centered Framework*. Tallahassee, FL: Nubian Nation Publications, 1992.

Kotkin, Joel. *Tribes: How Race, Religion and Identity Determine Success in the New Global Economy*. New York: Random House, 1992.

Mellon, James, ed. *Bullwhip Days-The Slaves Remember: An Oral History*. New York: Avon Books, 1988.

Richards, Dona Marimba. *Let The Circle Be Unbroken: The Implications of African Spirituality in the Diaspora*. Lawrenceville, NJ: Red Sea Press, 1989.

Some', Malidoma Patrice. *Of Water and the Spirit: Ritual, Magic, and Initiation in the Life of an African Shaman*. New York: GP Putnam & Sons, 1994.

_____. *Ritual: Power, Healing and Community*. Portland, OR: Swan Raven & Co., 1993.

This PART!!

To *every thing there is a season, and a time to every purpose
under the heaven:*

*A time to be born, and a time to die; a time to plant, and a time
to pluck up that which is planted;*

*A time to kill, and a time to heal; a time to break down, and a
time to build up;*

*A time to weep, and a time to laugh; a time to mourn, and a time
to dance;*

*A time to cast away stones, and a time to gather stones
together; a time to embrace, and a time ·to refrain from embracing;*

*A time to get, and a time to lose; a time to keep, and a time to
cast away;*

*A time to rend, and a time to sew; a time to keep silence, and a
time to speak;*

*A time to love, and a time to hate; a time of war, and a time of
peace.*

Ecclesiastes 3:1-8

STEP 12.

Learn to Prepare Yourself for War and Peace

A clear evaluation of Steps 1 through 11 should lead you to the understanding that Africans in America have been living in a state of war for over 350 years. This condition was blatantly obvious during the period of enslavement when our ancestors were brutalized. However, since emancipation, our ancestors have lived under the illusion of freedom while continuing to be brutalized by the local, state, and federal authorities. Physical enslavement was outlawed but economic, social, and psychological terrorism continued for over 100 years.

Even though contemporary Africans in America may not see "the rockets red glare" or feel the lash of the whip, we continue to live in a state of war. Warfare takes on many forms and there are numerous ways to neutralize an adversary. They can be subdued by: low intensity warfare, psychological warfare, germ warfare, chemical warfare, drug warfare, cultural warfare, infanticide, genocide, and mentacide (induced madness). Not all wars are fought in order to destroy an opponent, sometimes the objective is to simply terrorize them, or to contain and exploit them.

One of the most damaging forms of attack is spiritual warfare because it is strategically designed to destroy the soul of its victims and render them more easily susceptible to other forms of non-lethal assaults. In light of the historical relationship between Africans and Europeans in America, it is incumbent on Africans to understand the politics and psychology of warfare. Two thousand years ago, a Chinese philosopher named Sun Tzu wrote *The Art of War*, a book outlining the physical and spiritual nature of warfare. In it, the author presents an analysis of conflicts and resolutions which transcend time, culture, and ethnicity.

The writings of Sun Tzu have influenced political and military strategists, business persons, and human beings from all walks of life. I have highlighted Sun Tzu's suggestions on how to fight a war and win. I have also modified them to fit the context of this Step. Evaluate each statement and incorporate them into your survival strategies.

USE THIS AS A GUIDE!! FOR LIFE ......

1. Know your objectives! You must always have a clear vision or goal, or your life will have no purpose. This philosophy is reflected in the African proverb, "If you don't know where you are going, any road will take you there."

2. Develop a plan! Your plan should consist of the strategies and methods that you will employ to achieve your vision or accomplish your goal. While many people have goals, most lack the planning and discipline required to achieve their goals.

3. Master deep knowledge! The nature of the universe is to seek balance and harmony in every relationship. An understanding of universal forces and their impact on human behavior yields a profound level of awareness. It is believed that if one masters the laws of nature and human behavior, then your knowledge base will be increased by a factor of 10,000. If a picture is worth 1,000 words, then deep knowledge is worth 1,000 pictures.

4. Become invincible! The key to invincibility means that you must know and understand your enemy better than your enemy knows and understands you. You must study their thoughts and behavior, and never underestimate their abilities.

5. Be invisible! You should keep your plans secret until the moment you're ready to implement them. You must play your cards close to your chest and not draw attention to yourself by your words or actions until you are ready to strike.

6. Move with all deliberate speed! Speed has been defined as the art of being quick but not being in a hurry. To move swiftly, you must be conscious and confident of your every move.

7. Be strong! You must develop physical strength through exercise and mental strength through study. The body and mind must work in concert if you are going to achieve success in your endeavors.

8. Strive to win without fighting! It is always best to win a war by not fighting one. Learning how to problem solve and troubleshoot is one of the best ways to nip problems in the bud before they fester into unconquerable obstacles. However, if problems or conflicts do arise, you must move to resolve them quickly and efficiently.

THIS PART!! !

Those skilled in the martial arts learn techniques which can cause serious injury or even kill a person. They are also taught a philosophy which instills within them an understanding that they are to use these skills for self-defense. Thus, the power to take a life is balanced by a philosophy that instills a respect for life. What we now refer to as the martial arts were first developed by Buddhist monks in India around 400 B.C.E. These techniques were used by the monks to defend themselves against wild animals and later developed as a means of self-defense against humans in societies were weapons were outlawed.

Martial arts in the United States were popularized by the media, particularly the television series, *Kung-Fu*, which aired in the early 1970s. The lead character in the show was a Buddhist monk, of Chinese and European American ancestry, who fled to California after he committed a murder in China. The story takes place in the late 1800s as the fugitive monk searches for his American father, while avoiding bounty hunters, racists, and other thugs. The priest only uses his fighting skills as a last resort and relies heavily on the philosophical lessons he learned as a youth in the monastery to avoid conflicts.

Each week, the monk in *Kung-Fu* was able to overcome numerous adversaries because he was able to defend himself, and he possessed a spiritual system and a philosophy that allowed him to survive in a hostile environment. The priest preferred to live peacefully, but he was able to wage war when necessary. The survival strategies of the fictitious priest in *Kung-Fu* were no different from the tactics used by the groups mentioned in the book *Tribes* in Step 11. There are beneficial lessons to be learned even from a television series.

Africans in America and on the continent have been conditioned by their former enslavers and colonizers to wage war against each other and struggle nonviolently against their common oppressor. By accepting foreign values, philosophies, and religious ideologies, we have distanced ourselves from the spiritual teachings that sustained us through centuries of struggle.

Familiarity with African spiritual and philosophical concepts is an important step if we are to learn to make peace with ourselves and our communities. [Those who have never known peace are often possessed by a restless spirit that prevents them, and those in their environment, from ever knowing peace.\ When people become

[7 MY PEACE IS NON-NEGOTIABLE!.

centered and balanced, they are capable of experiencing peace and developing a greater appreciation of themselves and the world around them. Being at peace does not necessarily mean that a person is incapable or unwilling to defend himself. On the contrary, when a person knows peace, he or she will do anything to maintain it. Police officers and sheriffs were called "peace makers" for a reason, and they also carried a "piece" in order to maintain the peace.

There is no nation on Earth that had known peace longer than that of ancient Kemet. It has influenced and inspired the world for over 5,000 years. If we look into her past, we will find information which can be useful to us today. Kemet was formally established after an act of war, around 3150 B.C.E., when King Narmer united the two lands of Upper and Lower Kemet. This nation sustained itself for over 2,500 years, longer than any other in history, because it made peace its highest priority.

Maat (truth, justice, balance, harmony, etc.) was the embodiment of peace and the goal of every person in the land. It was believed that on the day of judgment, the heart of every person would have to be weighed on the scale of justice, opposite the feather of Maat. The soul would declare its innocence before Ausar and a panel of Netcherw. On that day, the soul would say: "I have not robbed. I have not stolen. I have done no murder. I have not spoken lies," and thirty-eight other Declarations of Innocence.

The nation of Kemet was sustained by a spirit which proclaimed Maat to be the moral standard against whom every person would be judged on Earth and in the afterlife. The population was encouraged to "think Maat, speak Maat, and do Maat." In order to achieve everlasting life, they had to become Maat. With that level of devotion, the people of Kemet established the greatest documented civilization which has ever existed. Imhotep, whose name means, "He who Comes In Peace," designed the first building of stone in 2630 B.C.E. He lived a life so remarkable that he is still regarded as the world's first multi-genius. The pyramids, temples, and tombs of Kemet were all labors of love, built, not by slave labor, but skilled engineers and artisans who put their hearts into their work.

Within Kemetic society, there was no separation between church and state, or the secular and the sacred. The rulers of this land were priestly kings who were instructed in all of the sacred literature. Many of them were given names which revealed their desire to attain a level of peace or contentment (*hotep*) with a specific Netecherw. There were four kings named *Amenhotep* and *Mentuhotep*, a prince named *Rahotep* and a host of other rulers and courtiers whose names expressed a special relationship with the Divine.

There also existed in Kemet a body of sacred literature which profoundly influenced the Torah, the Bible and the Quran. *The Instructions of Ptahhotep*, which is considered to be the oldest book in the world, consists of thirty-seven precepts of morality and ethics and was written over 4500 years ago. Books of instruction were written for royalty so that they would possess the wisdom to govern in the best interest of the people. *Ru Pert-em-Hru*, ("The Book of Coming Forth by Day") currently referred to as *The Book of the Dead*, is a collection of prayers, offerings, and moral instructions written to guide the souls of the deceased to *Amenta* (heaven). They were written on papyrus and buried with a body or they were carved in stone inside a burial chamber.

There exists within ancient and modern Africa literature, volumes of writings which can be of benefit to a mind seeking peace and harmony today. Wise instruction is food for a hungry soul, and it gives meaning and purpose to life. It makes life worth living and dying for. |A drum major for peace once commented, "If a man has not found a cause worth dying for, then he has not found a reason to live."| ⟶ i.e. Purpose!!

Most Africans in America have obtained their moral values from the scriptures of those who were once their slave masters. Christianity and Islam were both imposed on Africans by foreign invaders, but the acceptance of these two religions did not present a major problem, because both were similar to spiritual traditions that had been practiced in Africa thousands of years before they were introduced.

It certainly is not necessary to reject these religious teachings, because they have much to offer us. We should continue to read the Bible, and the Quran, and similar texts, but we should also study the sacred literature which influenced them.

There are three publications I would recommend for your spiritual enlightenment. They are translations of Kemetic texts, with a commentary which facilitates understanding:

1. *Selections From The Husia: Sacred Wisdom of Ancient Egypt.*

2. *The Book of Coming Forth by Day: The Ethics of the Declarations of Innocence.*

3. *The Teachings of Ptahhotep: The Oldest Book in the World.*

Additional RESOURCES

TO EXPLORE FOR
DEEPER UNDERSTANDING!!

References and Suggested Readings

Hilliard, III, Asa G., Williams, Larry and Damali, Nia. *The Teachings of Ptahhotep: The Oldest Book in the World*. Atlanta, GA: Blackwood Press, 1987.

Karenga, Maulana. *Selections From The Husia: Sacred Wisdom of Ancient Egypt*. Los Angeles, CA: The University of Sankore Press, 1984.

____. *The Book of Coming Forth by Day: The Ethics of the Declarations of Innocence*. Los Angeles, CA: The University of Sankore Press, 1990.

Sawyer, Ralph D. *The Art of War*. New York: Barnes & Noble, 1994.

Toffler, Alvin, and Heidi. *War and Anti-War: Survival At The Dawn Of The 21st Century*. Boston and New York: Little, Brown And Company, 1993.

. . . [T]he Negro is a sort of seventh son, born with a veil, and gifted with second-sight in this American world,—a world which yields him no true self-consciousness, but only lets him see himself through the revelation of the other world. It is a peculiar sensation, this double-consciousness, this sense of always looking at one's self through the eyes of others, of measuring one's soul by the tape of a world that looks on in amused contempt and pity. One ever feels his twoness,—an American, a Negro; two souls, two thoughts, two unreconciled strivings; two warring ideals in one dark body, whose dogged strength alone keeps it from being torn asunder.

The history of the American Negro is the history of this strife,—this longing to attain self-conscious manhood, to merge his double self into a better and truer self. In this merging he wishes neither of the other selves to be lost. He would not Africanize America, for America has too much to teach the world and Africa. He would not bleach his Negro soul in a flood of white Americanism, for he knows that Negro blood has a message for the world. He simply wishes to make it possible for a man to be both a Negro and an American. Without being cursed and spit upon by his fellows, without having the doors of opportunity closed roughly in his face.

The Souls of Black Folk
W.E.B. DuBois

STEP 13.

Learn How to Live in the New America

In recent years, I have had the opportunity to travel and lecture throughout the United States and three continents. I can say, with absolute certainty, despite its numerous shortcomings, America is one of the best places in the world to live at this time in history. Despite the ever-present specter of racism and white supremacy in this country, Africans in America are the wealthiest and best-educated African people on Earth. Despite negative images that are continually perpetuated in the media, Africans in America remain a consistent source of inspiration for people of color throughout the world.

Africans on the continent and those in Europe and Asia, look to Africans in America with a profound sense of awe and reverence. They know that our ancestors came to America in chains, they witnessed our struggle for liberation in the 1960s, and they see how we have excelled in areas where we were once excluded just two generations ago. Africans in America represent hope for the world. It is this hope that motivates many foreigners to leave their own homes and travel to America in search of a new life.

Let us not fool ourselves, however. Despite all of our accomplishments, Africans in America are sleeping giants; we have yet to reach our full potential. The dilemma of "double-consciousness" to which Du Bois referred almost a hundred years ago, is still a frightening reality and, from all indications, the problem of the "color line" will continue to plague us in the twenty-first century. Africans can achieve success in America, but we must develop the same "dogged strength" which enabled our ancestors to survive hardships much worse than we can ever imagine.

The history of America begins with a group of people who came to this country in search of freedom and were willing to steal, murder, and enslave others in order to achieve it. The Pilgrims were motivated by a vision and were willing to do anything to achieve it. America's Founding Fathers represent one of the clearest examples of a people fulfilling the vision of their ancestors. This nation now stands as the preeminent symbol of freedom and liberty in the world. It is a position held despite America's sordid past.

Many nations have sought to attain the level of success that America has achieved in such a relatively short period of time. I believe that one of the keys to America's success can be found by studying the demonstration in Step 8 where a person is lifted out of a chair by four individuals. The success of that demonstration required that all the participants *saw* themselves working in harmony in order to accomplish a common goal. They were given a vision and a plan of empowerment that allowed them to complete a seemingly impossible task. If we reexamine the vision and the plan of America's Founding Fathers, we can begin to understand the power that exists within African Americans and how it must be re-directed.

Immediately after the founding of America in 1776, George Washington saw the need to create a symbol to represent the heart and soul of his new nation. Washington authorized a committee of artisans to design a Great Seal, and experts in heraldry, symbolism, masonry, and the numeric sciences were all involved in its creation. Three separate committees were formed and dissolved during the six years it took to complete the design.

The finished product which stands before us today as a monument to the *vision* of the Founding Fathers and to the *African spirit* which was incorporated in the Great Seal. Every component has symbolic significance and multiple meanings that can only be ascertained by employing the evaluative skills that were discussed in Step 5. Let us evaluate the Great Seal by adapting the "double consciousness" modality. We will see it first through a European conscious and then from the cultural perspective of an African.

The reverse of the Great Seal consists of two symbols, a pyramid and an eye encased in a triangle at the apex of the pyramid. The pyramid comprises thirteen courses of stone and each row represents one of the thirteen colonies. The Roman numerals at the base of the pyramid equal 1776, the year the thirteen colonies united as one nation. The inscription beneath the pyramid, *Novus Ordo Seclorum*, in Latin refers to the "New Order of Ages," which came into existence when this nation was founded.

Above the pyramid is an eye, which symbolizes God, whom Masons refer to as the "Great Architect of the Universe." The Latin inscription above the eye, *Annuit Coetptis*, means that God was pleased with the undertaking of the newly established nation. Thus, one nation was built out of many states, by master builders, with the approval of the greatest builder in the universe. This is the official United States interpretation of the reverse of the Great Seal.

If we interpret this same symbol through African eyes, it takes on a profoundly different meaning. All of the symbolism on the reverse of the Great Seal is of African origin. Pyramids are an African creation, which are found only in lands that have been occupied by ancient Africans. At last count, there were ninety-seven pyramids in Egypt, fifteen pyramids in The Sudan and about a dozen pyramids in Ethiopia. The only place outside of the continent of Africa where ancient pyramids can also be found is Mexico.

Numerous scholars have described the presence of Africans in Mexico as early as 1,000 B.C.E. Africans are believed to have come from the Nile Valley and navigated across the Atlantic Ocean in numerous sailing vessels. The ancient travelers who settled in Mexico are now referred to as the *Olmecs*. They are said to have introduced stone construction, astronomy, and religious concepts to the indigenous inhabitants. Two of the most popular works on this topic are, *They Came Before Columbus: The African Presence in America* by Dr. Ivan Van Sertima and *Unexpected Faces in America* by the late Dr. Alexander von Wuthenau.

The Olmecs built huge stone likenesses of themselves in a number of ceremonial temples and they are believed to have inspired the construction of pyramids in this hemisphere. The architectural accomplishments of ancient Africans is unparalleled in human history. They were the first builders of pyramids and they have left behind some of the greatest architectural monuments in the world. The presence of a pyramid on the Great Seal is a testament to the skills of the world's first stonemasons.

The eye above the pyramid represents the *Eye of Heru*, the son of the resurrected God, Ausar. This symbol was associated with the sun which was regarded as the "right eye of God." It represents the omnipresent eye of the Creator who exists above the Earth and witnesses every activity below.

This African centered interpretation of the symbols on the Great Seal also requires that we reexamine the Latin inscriptions which surround them. The words *Novus Ordo Seclorum* at the base of the pyramid have a very specific meaning. The word "Novus" means *new*, "Ordo" means *order*, and "Seclorum" means *secluded* or *hidden*. In so many words, this symbol is a declaration of the establishment of the United States of America as a *New Secret Order*, founded on principles that originated in Africa ages earlier.

The inscription above the pyramid, *Annuit Coeptis*, literally describes how America achieved its wealth. The word "Annuit" means something that is received *annually*, and "Coeptis" means *unlimited wealth*. Historically speaking, the "unlimited wealth which was received annually," and made this nation great, came not from God, but from the free labor of enslaved Africans.

Imagine enslaving tens of millions of men, women, and children and working them from sun up to sun down, from birth until death. Imagine not having to pay these people for their labor and being allowed, by law, to rape and breed them in order to increase their numbers for your personal benefit. Imagine these conditions lasting for over three hundred years, and seeing your family accumulate a vast fortune that is passed on from generation to generation. Imagine no longer, because this is an American reality, and it is one aspect of the legacy of Africans in America.

The front of the Great Seal of the United States is the emblem you see on the podium whenever the President speaks, and it symbolizes the spirit of America. Let us examine the literal interpretation of this symbol as described by agencies of the Federal Government.

The eagle on the Great Seal holds an olive branch (symbol of peace) in the right talon, and arrows (symbols of war) in the left. The eagle looks to its right because the establishment of the nation was preceded by war, but it favors peace. The shield (escutcheon) on the breast of the eagle symbolizes self-reliance and the thirteen stripes represent the flag, which was created in 1777. In the eagle's beak is a banner with the Latin inscription *E pluribus unum*, which means *one* (nation) *out of many* (states). Above the eagle's head is a cluster of thirteen stars, which also represents the new nation that is protected by God.

If we examine the front of the Great Seal from an African centered point of view, we will find that it is imbued with many layers of symbolic imagery. As we unveil each layer, greater understanding is revealed. An analysis of the first layer reveals the African origin of the Great Seal. The representation of a bird holding symbolic implements was derived from an image of Heru which was created in ancient Kemet. One such design was found among the treasures of Tutankhamon, who died around 1325 B.C.E., approximately 2,107 years before the Great Seal was designed.

Heru was the symbol of rulership and he also represented an aspect of the sun that was a metaphor for God. Since the falcon had dominion over the sky, it was associated with God, Heru, and the sun. The falcon was also the national symbol of Kemet. As mentioned previously, the eye above the pyramid on the reverse of the Great Seal, is the *Eye of Heru* and also represents the all-seeing eye of God.

The symbol of Heru as a falcon holds a *shen* in each talon. There is an *ankh* above each shen and a sun disc above the head of Heru. The shen represents eternity, the ankh represents life, and the sun disc represents God. Heru looks to his right, which is symbolic of the future and his left symbolizes the past. This symbol means that when the light of God enters the mind of Heru, he is capable of living for eternity and transmitting life to the king, the nation, and its subjects.

When we analyze the second layer, we find a curious and repetitive pattern on the face of the Great Seal. The eagle holds in one claw an olive branch which has thirteen leaves and thirteen berries. In the other claw it holds thirteen arrows. The shield on the chest of the eagle has thirteen stripes. In its beak, the eagle grips a banner that is inscribed with the words *E pluribus unum*, which comprises thirteen letters. Above the eagle's head is a cluster of thirteen stars. This repetition of the number thirteen might lead one to conclude that the number thirteen must refer to the thirteen colonies. Right?

This conclusion is logical, but it is faulty considering that most people suffer from *triskaidekaphobia*, an unreasonable fear of the number thirteen. We should wonder why America was founded with thirteen colonies since we have been led to believe that thirteen is an unlucky number which has traditionally been associated with evil or death. Historically, *Friday the 13th* is an unlucky day. There are a number of buildings which lack a *13th floor*, and there are few theaters with *row 13*. Continental, Southwest and TWA airlines have rows of seats which are consecutively numbered, however, omitting *row 13*.

If thirteen is such an unlucky number, why is it repeated over and over on both sides of the Great Seal? Why was America founded with thirteen colonies instead of twelve? Why not ten colonies or fourteen? What is the true significance of the number thirteen? Analyzing the third layer from the Great Seal provides even deeper insight and answers to these important questions.

Eighteenth century Masons believed that their "craft" originated in Egypt and they strove, in every way, to replicate the greatness of that ancient civilization. Freemasonry played a major role in the early development of the United States--all thirty-three generals in the Revolutionary War were Masons, as were fifty of the fifty-six signers of the Declaration of Independence, and thirteen of the forty signers of the Constitution. Sixteen of the forty-two presidents of the United States have been Masons and four others were undocumented members.

Within the practice of Masonry, there exists a philosophy concerning the esoteric meaning of numbers. Each number represents profound concepts and ideas which are known and understood only by a select few. For example, the number *one* has traditionally been associated with God, The Creator. The number *two* represents the dual aspects of creation which are expressed as complementary opposites or male and female. The number *three* represents the union of man and woman which produces a child, an offspring. This is the Trinity as expressed by the eye in the triangle on the reverse of the Great Seal.

The number *four* symbolizes a foundation or base. It also represents the four points of the compass and the four sides of the pyramid which face North, East, West, and South. Each side is separate from the other, but if you climb to the top of the pyramid, all four sides come together. That is where the eye of God opens, and knowledge, or reason, is attained. The initials of the four directions--NEWS--represent a similar gathering of knowledge from the four directions which informs and enlightens. The number *five* represents man. This interpretation is devoid of gender, and comes from the Sanskrit word which literally means *mind*. According to this perspective, the word *woman* means the "womb that produces mind." The body of man comprises five basic parts: a head, two arms, and two legs. Man has five fingers, five toes and five senses. This is the reason why the flags of most nations have five pointed stars--they represent the people of that nation.

The number *six* is traditionally associated with death--the physical, mental, and spiritual death of man. That is the reason why "man" was buried in a coffin with six sides. The coffin was carried to the grave site by six pallbearers and was lowered six feet into the ground. This triple repetition of the number *six* (666) represents the physical, mental, and spiritual death of man.

The number *seven* represents man overcoming death and rising to heaven. This is the significance of the term *seventh heaven*. Seven is considered to be one of the most important symbolic numbers as it is the sum of the three and four. It embodies the combined significance of both numbers, that is, perfection.

The number *eight* is four doubled and represents the dual aspects of balance and stability on earth and in heaven. It also symbolizes the balance between the macrocosm and the microcosm, as expressed in the saying, "as above, so below."

The number *nine* represents the descent of divine power into the world. It is the number three (the trinity) multiplied by itself and embodies all of its highest attributes. In many traditions, prayers were offered three times a day because the day was divided into three parts--morning, noon, and night. In the Catholic tradition, the *Angelus*, a prayer commemorating the *Incarnation*, is offered three times a day, and the bell which pronounces it rings nine times. On the Great Seal, the nine tail feathers on the eagle represent the descent of the divine power to the United States.

Every number symbolizes profound concepts and ideas that most people know nothing about because they are trained to interpret numbers literally. They do not infer their deeper meaning or evaluate them based upon the historical and cultural significance and philosophies they represent in other cultures. The superstitions traditionally associated with numbers are an attempt by those in control of knowledge to camouflage their importance and make a mockery of the truth. The number *twelve* represents the completion of a cycle. The twelve months represent a complete year. Twelve hours of daylight plus twelve hours of nighttime, during the equinox, represent a complete day. The number *thirteen* symbolizes the energy from a completed cycle which has moved into a higher, spiritual state. Therefore, the number *thirteen* represents "transformation and rebirth," which is also regarded as the process of *spiritual transformation*. That is the real reason why America was founded with thirteen colonies. Thirteen represented the transformation and rebirth of the spirit of ancient Egypt in the New World Order.

The knowledge of the transformative nature of the number *thirteen* is not new and has been expressed many different ways throughout the centuries. There are twelve signs of the zodiac plus the sun, twelve persons in a jury plus the judge. There were twelve knights of the Round Table plus King Arthur, and at the Last Supper there were twelve disciples plus The Christ, who later died and was reborn. Every Christmas, millions of people throughout the world sing a carol about *The Twelve Days of Christmas*, and the Catholic Church celebrates the *Epiphany* (birth of Jesus) on January 6, the thirteenth day.

By putting a spin on the truth, people are conditioned to become oblivious to that which stares them in the face. The men who established the United Stated knew exactly what they were doing, and they were conscious that the number *thirteen* represented resurrection, rebirth, and new life. This nation was founded with thirteen colonies in 1776. Seven plus six equals *thirteen*. There is a slogan associated with this particular time in American history "The Spirit of '76" which represents *The Spirit of Spiritual Transformation*.

The birth date of America is July 4, 1776, which fell exactly thirteen days after the summer solstice which occurred on June 21st in the year 1776. The solstice is a day of profound significance within Freemasonry as well as Christianity. It refers to the four-day period when the "sun is still" and being spiritually transformed before it is reborn on the 25th of June and December.

The founders of the United States considered themselves men of reason who did not believe that man fell from grace. They were practicing deists who believed that man was capable of achieving the knowledge of God and obtaining the freedom to reason and learn. This was the basic principle of democracy, and it was accessible to any male in America as long as he was "free, white, and twenty-one."

When you add 1776 (one plus seven plus seven plus six), you get twenty-one, the age of reason and adulthood as acknowledged in the United States of America.

This is the essence of the founding of the United States, a nation conceived in sin, dedicated to the destruction of Native Americans, and the enslavement of African Americans. What has kept this nation from being torn asunder is the blanket of spiritual protection in which it has cloaked itself. The source of that protection is clearly identified on the Great Seal as an African spirit.

The founders of the United States were men of vision, who used the land of others and the labor and knowledge of others to make their vision a reality. They have sustained their position of power and authority over Africans in America by destroying the Africans' ability to *visualize* while encouraging them to *dream*.

There is a fundamental difference between a vision and a dream. Dreams are abstract illusions that occur when one is in an unconscious state of mind. Dreams dry up "like a raisin in the sun" and lead to frustration, anger, and despair. Visions occur during a state of heightened awareness and provide insight into areas where the mind is trained and focused. Visions are capable of connecting a mind to a higher source of consciousness and empowerment. This is a spiritual law which leads to the fulfillment of thoughts and ideas, and, therefore, happiness.

It has been written: "Where there is no vision, the people perish, but he that keepeth the law, happy is he." This statement implies that the quality of your life is directly proportional to your ability to develop a vision and implement it throughout your lifetime. If this is done correctly, the power of that vision will be projected into the future and manifested for generations to come.

The Creator has given each of us the power of *visualization*, so that we may create a world of our own design. This power is negated if it is not used correctly, and it will never be given to a people by a government or a religious system which once enslaved them. This message is of critical importance for Africans in America. Those who once enslaved you will never share their power, for fear that you will hate them as they have hated you. However, hatred and fear have no place in a mind which desires freedom because fear blocks spiritual blessings and hatred destroys them.

Africans in America must develop the desire and the ability to create a vision for our future. We must understand that every thought, every word, and every action which emanates from us will have an effect on the next seven generations--150 years into the future. Thoughts and words are more than a mere process of communication; they have the ability to manipulate consciousness and influence future events. What you say and do frames the consciousness of your children and directs them to use those same thoughts and ideas to frame the consciousness of their children.

Africans in America are in a unique position to access the physical resources of the most powerful nation on Earth to fulfill their vision. But time is of the essence. Within the next twenty-five years, Hispanics will become the largest minority in America, followed by Asians. Africans will then fall to the number three position among America's "minority" population, and if Africans have not achieved equity as the number one minority, it surly will not materialize in the number three slot.

We have no alternative but to look to ourselves for solutions. African Americans are standing at the crossroads, and we must carefully determine which road we will take into the twenty-first century. If we go to the left and riot out of fear and hatred, we will be wiped out by those forces in America waiting for an excuse to annihilate us. If we continue down the current road, and ignore the signposts that read "This way to re-enslavement," we will find ourselves enslaved to poverty, ignorance, crime, violence, alcohol, and drugs for generations to come. Africans in America have no alternative but to turn to our right, that is, return to our *right* minds. The path leads us to knowledge, power, self-consciousness, spiritual enlightenment, and freedom.

Rugged individualism has been the clarion call of American society since its earliest beginnings. Such a mindset leads to the belief that we do live in a "dog eat dog world." But, we are human beings not dogs, and we must demand a higher standard of living. In traditional African society is a belief in the need for mutual cooperation among all people in order for the group to exist. This idea is expressed in the philosophy, "I am because we are, and we are because I am."

In order for Africans in America to live meaningful lives, we must make a conscious effort to reverse the lingering effects of the dreaded Willie Lynch syndrome which has been implanted in the minds of Africans. The people of Ghana have a proverb which offers a viable solution to that dilemma: "The ruin of a nation begins in the home of its people." The converse of that statement does provide a meaningful course of action, "The salvation of our nation must begin in the homes of our people."

We must make a commitment to bring out the best within ourselves, not for our own selfish interest, but for the benefit of the group. Males must learn the responsibilities of manhood and live up to them every day of their lives. Females must cultivate virtues which will allow them to achieve true womanhood. We should not strive to become the caricatures who have been created for us by the media. Instead, we should aspire to become the embodiment of those ancestors who have opened doors for us and showed us the way.

When men and women come together with a conscious respect for themselves and their mates, they are better prepared to bring life into the world and direct it along the path to freedom. Consider the following guidelines for yourselves and your family.

1.   Develop a strong spiritual base upon which you can build your life.   Learn to respect life and the creative spirit which exists within each person. As you move out into society, remember the words of John Henrik Clarke who said, "Service is the highest form of prayer."

2. Learn to bring out the best within yourself so that you will be capable of bringing out the best in others. Value your history and culture, and keep your focus on education instead of entertainment.

3. Learn to think seven generations into the future, and begin today to establish the quality of life you wish for your descendants to live.

4. Every home should have a library of books and related materials by and about people of African descent. Time should be established for regular periods of study and discussion.

5. Monitor and restrict the use of television. It is not a baby-sitter and should not play a critical role in the life of children or adults.

6. Be cautious of the type of music that is listened to in your home. Rhythmic beats are the best way to deliver self-destructive thoughts into the mind and neutralize the creative spirit within us.

7. Patronize and support the cultural and financial institutions within the African American community. Spend your dollars with those who are committed to improving the quality of life in your neighborhoods.

8. The world is moving toward a service-oriented, computer-based society. Anyone who is not service-oriented and computer literate will have a difficult time living in the America of the twenty-first century. Buy a computer and learn to use it today!

9. Make study and the application of knowledge priorities in your life. The August 1996 issue of *Emerge* magazine featured two articles on African Americans and the information superhighway that underscore the importance of mastering information and technology. In his editorial, George Curry, editor-in-chief of *Emerge*, cautioned the reader of the threat posed by *Information 'Apartheid'* in the near future:

> Experts estimate that the sum total of human knowledge doubled from 1750 to 1900. It doubled again between 1900 and 1950, and yet again from 1950 to 1960. The same held true for 1960-65. By the year 2000, knowledge is projected to double every 73 days. And there's simply no way to compete in the future without mastering the computer, the instrument through which much of this knowledge will pass.

References and Suggested Readings

Kimbro, Dennis, and Hill, Napoleon. *Think and Grow Rich: A Black Choice,* New York: Fawcett Crest, 1991.

Madhubuti, Haki R. *Claiming Earth: Race, Rage, Rape, Redemption: Blacks Seeking a Culture of Enlightened Empowerment.* Chicago, IL: Third World Press, 1994.

Van Sertima, Ivan. *They Came Before Columbus.* New York: Random House, 1976.

Vanzant, Iyanla. *The Spirit of A Man: A Vision of Transformation for Black Men and the Women Who Love Them.* New York: HarperCollins Publishers, 1996.

Von Wuthenau, Alexander. *Unexpected Faces In Ancient America.* New York: Crown Publishers, 1982.

To achieve and maintain freedom you must learn to listen to your inner voice; this higher wisdom is always present within you.

Overcoming obstacles in life is easier when you are in tune with the infinite.

When seeking solutions to life's problems, remember that the answer can be found within the problem. Every new day is a new opportunity. Every ending is a new beginning. Your life is an endless unfolding.

When you change your mind you instantly change your relationship to time. An attitude is all you need to achieve freedom or to lose it.

Inspire yourself. Your life may be yours but your spirit belongs to the Creator.

The bird waits in the egg. The oak sleeps in the acorn, and the Creator awaits within you.

You gravitate to that which you secretly love most and you make in life the exact reproduction of your thoughts. There is no chance, coincidence or accident, in a universe ruled by law and divine order.

You rise as high as your dominant aspiration. You descend to the level of your lowest concept of yourself. Spirit has the answers, but its nature is to respond to your thoughts.

Be careful of the thought seeds you plant in the garden of your mind for seeds grow after they are cast.

Every thought felt as true, or allowed to be accepted as true by your conscious mind, takes root in your subconscious mind, blossoms sooner or later into an act, and bears its own fruit.

The fruit will not fall far from the tree. Good thoughts will produce good fruit. Bad thoughts will produce diseased seeds which will yield bitter fruit.

If you think right you will know freedom, and you will find paradise on earth. The choice is always yours to make.

As A Man Thinketh / Good Thoughts-Bad Thoughts

(James Allen, George Clinton & Tony Browder)

FREEDOM

As people mature they are given certain freedoms commensurate with their age. Time and space are the instruments used to determine when these freedoms will be dispensed, and your sense of responsibility dictates how long you will keep them.

- At 16 you receive a drivers license
- At 18 you can vote, drink and smoke
- At 21 you become an adult and receive greater degrees
  of freedom

The laws of society demand that you attain a certain level of maturity before your are granted specific freedoms. As you mature you learn that freedom is not free, it must be earned and diligently sustained. Freedom is more than the right to do what you want, when you want, simply because you can. The cemeteries, prisons, hospitals, and streets are full of people who did what they wanted to do, at great expense to themselves, their families, and innocent bystanders.

Freedom means little by itself; it must be tempered with knowledge, wisdom, and spiritual direction for it to be of lasting value. You should desire the freedom to access information which will allow you to make the best choices possible; not just for yourself, but for your family, your descendants, and for the planet. We are all in this world together, and the freedoms that we exercise determine whether we will make this world a heaven or a hell.

I have compiled the material in this book for people who were once denied freedom of movement, freedom of thought, and freedom of spiritual expression. It is my hope that you will now use this information to broaden your knowledge of African culture while simultaneously taking full advantage of all of the resources America has to offer.

Knowledge without action is meaningless. Freedom without direction is wasteful. Knowledge and freedom must be used in concert in order to achieve victory over the challenges which life poses. With a working knowledge of the spiritual laws that govern the universe, there are few challenges which cannot be overcome, and many which can be avoided.

You have the freedom to master the art of reading, thinking, and studying. Such activities strengthen the mind and make it less susceptible to negative influences. If you exercise your freedom to focus your mind on entertainment, at the expense of education, your mind, body, and spirit will suffer. The mind is similar to a muscle that atrophies when it is not used consistently. When the mind fails, the body will follow, but exercised regularly, the mind will serve you for a lifetime, and blessings will flow from within.

In order to truly prepare yourself for freedom, you must be conscious of the power of your thoughts and words. Whether you realize it or not, we are all affected by the universal principle of reciprocity. It is true that *what goes around, comes around.* You cannot speak ill of someone or cause them harm without expecting the same negative energies to return to you. It is a basic fact of life and understanding this will allow you to avoid a great many hardships.

You must be aware of your diet and exercise greater control over what and how often you eat. I believe wholeheartedly that soul food--ham hocks, bacon, fried foods, and foods high in sodium, are our greatest nutritional enemies. We must begin to eat foods that will nourish our bodies instead of catering to unnatural appetites promoted by the media. Ultimately, we must understand that everything we eat affects our body, mind, and spirit.

The body is the temple which houses our spirit. This means that the Creator lives within all of us. As a result of this spiritual connection, our bodies are the vessels through which creative power and creative spirit express themselves through our thoughts, words, and deeds. Our bodies will experience a diminished capacity to connect with the spirit if we are neglectful of its needs. Therefore, we must make certain that we obtain adequate rest, sufficient exercise, eat nutritious foods, and avoid drugs.

When we enter a mosque, church or temple, there is a certain decorum we are expected to maintain. We should adopt the same attitude concerning the temple which exists within our bodies. We should not do anything to our bodies, or the bodies of others, that would denigrate the spirit that dwells within. We must understand that everything that happens to us serves as a barometer which allows us to measure the flow of spiritual energy within and around us. The quality of our relationships, the quality of our health, and the quality of our finances are just a few of the indicators which alert us to the quality of the spiritual energy within us.

If we experience frequent periods of distress, illness, or what some may call bad luck, this is because our spiritual energy is out of balance, and we are attracting an abundance of negative energy. There is no such thing as bad luck, *chance, coincidence or accident in a universe which is ruled by law and divine order.* This universal order was referred to as *Maat* by the ancient Africans in the Nile Valley.

Maat was the personification of the forces of *truth, justice, balance, harmony, order, righteousness,* and *reciprocity.* She was the standard against which every soul was judged. Awareness of these principles, and the obligation to declare their application on the day of judgment were sufficient inducement to think and act correctly throughout one's life. There was no need for Commandments.

If you are experiencing difficulties in your life, then you must take the time to evaluate your thoughts and behavior. You must examine the energies you have set in motion which are now boomeranging and causing complications. If you assess situations correctly, you will have the knowledge to remedy the problem and plot a new course of action.

I believe that a positive change in your life can be initiated by setting aside thirty minutes each day for personal introspection. Thirty minutes are not excessive when you consider the average person spends eight hours a day at work, two hours preparing for work, two hours returning from work, and about eight hours sleeping. That adds up to approximately twenty hours per day that is usually spent fulfilling someone else's requirement of you.

How much time do we take for ourselves to evaluate where we are in our lives and where we need to be? If you allow just thirty minutes a day, which can be divided into fifteen minute segments in the morning and evening, you can begin to balance your energies and focus your mind. You begin by reviewing the day's activities, assessing your successes and failures, and developing strategies to implement any changes.

Let's say you have a habit of speaking ill about your family, co-workers, or friends, and you wish to make a conscious effort to eliminate any negative thoughts. Tell yourself, "Negative thoughts are harmful to me and the people to whom I direct them.

I will exercise greater control over my thoughts and my words." As you think these thoughts, you will become more conscious of your speech. After a short while, you will notice that people will begin to respond to you differently.

Once you have succeeded in controlling the frequency of your negative thoughts, you can begin to focus on other areas of importance. The objective of this exercise is to train your mind to be responsive to your thoughts and desires, and allow your spirit to influence your thoughts. Remember, this is the idea associated with Her-em-akhet, the statue you once referred to as the Sphinx. If you will allow spirit to influence your mind, you will begin to control the beast within.

As you process each day's activity, you must also devise a plan of action for the following day. If you see that you are doing something correctly, you would want to duplicate that success the following day. If you see that you've done something that warrants correcting, you must analyze your behavior so that you will correct the specific problems on the following day. Always plan for tomorrow, and while you analyze your thoughts, be fair and honest with yourself, but also be firm and diligent.

The third component of your thirty minutes a day regimen requires setting aside some time for quiet prayer, meditation, and reflection. Everyone needs some time to know him/herself and connect with one's inner spirit. Prayer is when you talk to the Creator. Meditation is when the Creator talks to you. Reflection is when you are conscious that this dialogue can and does take place. It is only by being still and calming the mind that you can begin to hear, understand, and follow the directions of that *clear voice* within you. Know yourself and allow spirit to guide you through your journey in life.

With serious devotion you will find that most personal challenges can be overcome in as little as twenty-eight days. Why twenty-eight days? It takes approximately four weeks to eliminate negative thought patterns and implement new ones, (Remember that seven is the number of perfection, and four represents a foundation.) If you use these guidelines for thirty minutes a day, for twenty-eight consecutive days, you will begin the process of mastering your life and enjoying the freedom that it brings.

The Chinese have a proverb to instill faith and devotion to all who understood its meaning: "The journey of a thousand miles begins with the first step." Remember this proverb as you apply the *13 Steps To Freedom* in your daily life. Each Step you take will lead you out of the shadow of racism and white supremacy and one step closer to freedom. These are your *13 Steps To Freedom*. Share them with your family and friends and teach them to your children. Take each step carefully, move with all deliberate speed and enjoy your journey.

References and Suggested Readings

Allen, James. *As A Man Thinketh*. Marina Del Rey, CA: DeVorss Publications,

Chopra, Deepak. *The Seven Spiritual Laws of Success: A Practical Guide To the Fulfillment of Your Dreams*. San Rafael, CA: Amber-Allen Publishing & New World Library, 1994.

Copage, Eric V. *Black Pearls: Daily Meditations, Affirmations, and Inspirations for African-Americans*. New York: William Morrow and Company, 1993.

Taylor, Susan L. *In the Spirit: The Inspirational Writings of Susan L. Taylor*. New York: HarperCollins, 1993.

Vanzant, Iyanla. *Acts of Faith: Daily Meditations for People of Color*. New York: Fireside, 1993.

Survival Strategies For Africans In America
13 Steps To Freedom

M I N D

STEP 1.   Racism and White Supremacy Are the Most
           Persistent Problems Confronting Africans in America

STEP 2.   Become Aware of the Power of the Media

STEP 3.   Perception Precedes Being . . . You Are Who You
           Believe You Are

STEP 4.   Information Is Power, But Power Is Nothing
           Without Control

STEP 5.   Empower Your Mind . . . See the World Through
           African Eyes

B O D Y

STEP 6.   Become Aware of the Uniqueness of Your African Body

STEP 7.   Develop Cultural and Holistic Approaches to Health

STEP 8.   Become Aware of Your Mind/Body Relationships

STEP 9.   Familiarize Yourself with the Mysteries of Melanin

S P I R I T

STEP 10.   Learn to Interpret Religious Imagery

STEP 11.   Learn to Honor the Memory of Your Ancestors

STEP 12.   Learn to Prepare Yourself for War and Peace

STEP 13.   Learn How to Live in the New America

Afterword

Every Ending Is A New Beginning

As I conclude this final chapter of *Survival Strategies*, I wish to stress the importance of finding a culturally-centered value system to help you navigate the waters of life. The difficulties in life challenge us to find ways to survive and move to higher levels of comfort and consciousness. We must do this for ourselves and for those whom we love. By virtue of the fact that we are born into this world, we are continually faced with one common inevitability--death, the great equalizer. Learning to understand how to deal with this critical step in the life cycle is important if we are to make the most out of our daily lives.

On September 11, 1996, the grand matriarch of my family, Mary Elizabeth Walker, my grandmother, made her earthly transition. As the first grandchild in our immediate family, I was compelled to share the remembrances of my grandmother at her funeral services. My thoughts were cathartic and struck a harmonious cord with our family and friends. I sought my family's permission to include those remarks in this publication for the benefit of our larger cultural family, and as a living memorial of one we loved so dearly. I am grateful to my family for their consent, their belief in me, and confirmation of my work.

Mary E. Walker's Homegoing
September 16, 1996

As the first grandchild of Eddie and Mary Walker, I was more blessed than some of the other grandchildren in the family to have known them in many ways. I would like to take some time this morning to share my thoughts of my grandparents with you, the other members of the family and the friends who have gathered here to pay their respect to our grandmother.

I lived in the same household with my grandparents for the first five years of my life. And then I lived upstairs above them, in their home at 3225 W. Walnut Street in Chicago, for another seven years.

I can say—beyond a shadow of a doubt—that my interactions with my grandparents throughout my early life, shaped my personality and helped make me the person I am today.

The spirit of creativity I possess, my love of animals, and my sense of pride were instilled in me by my grandfather.

• I helped him build fences, bookcases, a doghouse, and other items around the house.

• We used to walk to Garfield Park, and feed bread crumbs to the ducks. (That was back in the days when it was safe to walk in the park during the daylight hours.)

• He was fiercely proud of his African and Native American heritage. (He never responded favorably to the word *Negro* and he always wrote the word "other" when asked to identify his race on any form or application.)

My sense of compassion, love of nature, and belief in a creative spirit were programmed into my consciousness by my grandmother.

• She always had a kind word for everyone regardless of how they treated her.

- Each spring I dug up the front yard and helped her plant flowers--marigolds, zinnias, and gladioli, and we watered them and weeded them all summer long until the last flower died in the fall.

- I saw my grandmother pray every day, several times a day. And she always prefaced any plans for the future with the phrase *"If the Lord permits."*

Loving memories of my grandparents will remain in my heart all my life. Especially when my memories of them are challenged by this thing called death.

I can remember sitting in this church during my grandfather's funeral on April 22, 1967 and feeling an emptiness that I had never known before. I set there thinking that death was the worse pain any person could ever endure.

I wanted to know how I could learn to live with death since I knew that I would have to face it many times throughout my lifetime. I sought to understand this human inevitability and learn not to fear something which is as natural as life itself.

I have pondered this issue throughout the years, and then, last Wednesday, when my mother told me that my grandmother had passed, I felt a sense of relief and I said, "I'm glad. I'm glad that she doesn't have to suffer any longer. I'm glad that she's at peace."

As I reflect on the differences in my reaction to the passing of each of my grandparents, I now realize, and appreciate how much I have grown over the last twenty-nine years.

I now realize that death is not an end--it's just a new beginning.

I realize how important our beliefs are, but I also know how important it is to reinforce our beliefs with understanding.

I've found that if you believe in something without understanding why you believe in it, you will become very confused.

A belief is like a seed, which, when planted in our mind, takes root in our subconscious and blossoms into thoughts. Every belief must be nourished by the waters of understanding for it to grow into a healthy thought. Without understanding, a belief just sits in our mind, clouding our thoughts.

Allow me to illustrate my point.

As a youngster, there were times when I believed that my grandfather was the angriest man on earth. He had a temper and he was the only person I knew who could cuss for ten minutes straight and never use the same swear word twice.

Every day my grandfather would find something new to cuss about before he left the house for work. He also had this habit of calling my grandmother "Girl!"

He'd tell her, "Girl, fix me some coffee." She would make the coffee, and then he would complain, "Girl, why did you make the coffee so strong?" or "Girl, why did you make the coffee so hot?" He would take a sip of the coffee, pour the rest down the drain, and leave for work.

I was at a loss to explain his behavior. Thus, I believed that he truly was the angriest man on earth. As a child, I also believed that my grandfather called my grandmother "Girl" because she was a female. Since my grandfather was a male, I believed that it was all right for me to call him "Boy." And so I did. My grandmother also called him "Boy," a nickname which stuck with him for the rest of his life.

Twenty years later, as an adult, after my grandfather had passed, I began to understand the source of his anger. I realized that it was *displaced anger*. You see, my grandfather lived in a time when discrimination and prejudice ran rampant throughout America. If you were a black man, with a limited education, trying to find employment in a racist society, you were faced with very few promising job prospects. You see, they didn't have equal employment opportunities or civil rights back in the days when my grandfather was raising his family.

So, imagine this man, my grandfather, with a wife, seven children, a grandchild, and a house note. Imagine this man trying to feed, clothe and provide shelter for his family. Imagine him living in a society where his manhood was never respected because of the color of his skin.

You will find that it is difficult to imagine yourself in my grandfather's shoes without becoming a little angry yourself. Pressure will do that to you, and unrelenting pressure will affect you in ways that you cannot even imagine.

So my grandfather was quick to anger, and he brought this anger home and projected his frustrations on to his wife.

- He couldn't be the boss at work, so he wanted to be boss at home.
- He called my grandmother "Girl" at home, because he was called "Boy" at work.

My grandfather was not born a mean person. He was a wonderful man who found it difficult to express love to his family because he was constantly beaten down throughout his life. The pressures of society affected his behavior and health, and ultimately influenced his relationship with his family.

Now my grandmother was able to deal with all of this because she was a deeply religious woman who believed in God and found comfort in the church. She was also an incredibly spiritual woman whose soul was immune from the hypocrisy which possessed the hearts of so many people who went to church on Sunday and acted like heathens as soon as they walked through of the doors of the church.

You know the type of people that I'm talking about. They're the ones who sit up in church and say that they love the Lord and can't stand the person sitting next to them.

My grandmother knew that sort of behavior wasn't correct and she wasn't a hypocrite. Of all the years that I spent in the company of my grandmother, I never once heard her swear and I never saw her turn her back on anyone who needed help.

There was a spirit in my grandmother which I saw continually manifesting itself throughout her marriage with my grandfather. There was a presence within her which neutralized the anger and pain that my grandfather brought home every day.

My grandmother filled our house with a spirit of love that flowed out of the windows, through the doors, all up and down Walnut Street.

My Grandmother's spirit followed us as we walked out of the house to Beidler Elementary School or traveled to Marshall High School.

My Grandmother's spirit stayed with my family even after they moved out of the house to the South Side of Chicago or further West. Her spirit traveled with them when they moved to Markham, Oak Park and Maywood.

Her spirit guided and protected us when we moved to Ithaca, New York, Washington, D.C., Dallas, Texas, and San Diego, California.

Throughout our lives, Mama's spirit has never left us. Even when she was confined to a wheel chair and after she entered the nursing home, her spirit was with us always.

In recent years as she moved in and out of the hospital and lapsed in and out of a coherent state of mind, her spirit was still with us. Even though she was not always physically or mentally present, she was always spiritually by our side.

Now that she has made her physical transition, I want you to know that *spiritually*, she will never leave us to ourselves.

The pride of my heritage, which I inherited from my grandfather, and the love of spirit, which I inherited from my grandmother, encouraged me to seek knowledge of my African roots. And I have grown from that experience.

My understanding of African history and culture has taught me that *spirit* is the most important aspect of being. This physical body is temporary. It was only designed to last for a limited period of time. It may be 59 years, as in the case of my grandfather, or 85 years as it was for my grandmother. It could be any number in between those two ages, or any number before or after.

This physical body is temporary, but it is designed to contain a spirit which will last forever.

We don't know how long we will have our bodies, but we must understand that our spirits are eternal. When we leave our bodies behind, and become ancestors, we must understand that our spirits are always assessable to those we have left behind. *We, the living, are never alone.*

Our traditions remind us that spirit is the link to our past and also a bridge to our future, but those links and bridges are only as strong as we make them today. Spirit links our ancestors, us, and our descendants in one grand circle which binds us together as one family and one people. This circle must never be broken.

Before our people were enslaved and became Negroes, trained to believe in the traditions of their slave masters, *our people, black people, African people* knew that as long as we spoke the name of the deceased, they would continue to live in our hearts and minds.

Our people knew that as long as we left a light on, our ancestors would come visit us. As long as we left a chair, they would come and sit with us. As long as we left a plate for them at the table, they would dine with us. As long as we poured libation for them, they would drink with us. Black people knew that we were inextricably linked to our ancestors. That's why we could talk with them and not be considered crazy by our family members. My grandmother told me that she talked to her father, Papa Felix, all the time.

This admission let me know that it was all right for me to talk with my grandfather after he became an ancestor. I have talked to him regularly since 1981. With his direction, I have been able to run a successful design business, which has allowed me to develop a career as a writer, lecturer, and researcher.

His guidance has help me travel all over the world while remaining self-employed for almost twenty years. With my grandfather's spirit by my side, I will never have to worry about working for white people ever again, or working in a hostile environment with people who will abuse me and cause me to abuse my family. That will never happen.

I talked to my grandfather recently and asked him to give me the strength to stand before you today. I talked with my grandmother last Friday and asked her to give me the words to speak when I stood before you.

The person that you see standing here is not alone. I am just a reflection of the spirit of my grandmother, my grandfather, and all of the ancestors who came before me.

My grandmother is here. My grandfather is there. Mama Clarence, Uncle Marshall, Aunt Earlene, Uncle Fred, Cousin Turk-- they're all in front of me, running interference, removing obstacles and paving a way for me, and all of the family, *I know this to be true.*

Their spirit has taught me the meaning of *sankofa.*

I now understand that we have the right to reclaim the past, the ability to correct the mistakes of the past, and that we are charged with the responsibility to build a future for ourselves and all of those who will come behind us.

I understand that we can do all of these things with the help of God, who works through the spirits of our ancestors, and that we can *initiate* these ancestral relationships whenever we are ready and as often as we are willing.

I understand that our ancestors are not gone and that they are waiting for us to acknowledge their spirits and invite them back into our lives.

I thank you grandma for helping me to understand these realities and I will always be grateful to you for the lessons you've taught me. I'll love you eternally, and I'll be talking with you soon.

Until then, I bid you good night and pray that you get the rest that you truly deserve.

Mary Elizabeth Walker
December 31, 1910 - September 11, 1996

Anthony and Atlantis Browder

About the Author

Anthony T. Browder is an author, publisher, cultural historian, artist, and an educational consultant. He is a graduate of Howard University's College of Fine Arts and has lectured extensively throughout the United States, Africa, Caribbean, Mexico, Japan and Europe, on issues related to African and African American History and Culture.

Mr. Browder is the founder and director of IKG Cultural Resources and has devoted 30 years researching ancient Egyptian history, science, philosophy and culture. He has traveled to Egypt 47 times since 1980 and is currently director of the ASA Restoration Project which is funding the excavation and restoration of the 25th dynasty tomb of Karakhamun in Luxor, Egypt. Browder is the first African American to fund and coordinate an archeological dig in Egypt and has lead five archeological missions to Egypt since 2009.

Mr. Browder's three decades of study have lead him to the conclusion that ancient Africans were the architects of civilization and developed the rudiments of what has become the scientific, religious, and philosophical backbone of mankind. It is from this framework that IKG has concentrated its research and disseminated its findings.

Through IKG, Mr. Browder sponsors lectures, seminars, cultural field trips of Washington, D.C., publishes his research, and has conducted study tours to Egypt, West Africa, South Africa and Mexico since 1987.

He is the author of six publications (including the best sellers, From the Browder File and Nile Valley Contributions to Civilization) and the co-author of four publications, including two written with his now 29-year-old daughter, Atlantis Tye. All of Mr. Browder's publications are currently being used in classrooms around the world.

"Tony" is an autodidact and describes himself a chronicler of facts and information relative to the positive portrayal of the worldwide African experience.

For information on speaking engagements contact IKG at:
301-853-2465 or online at www.ikg-info.com

FROM THE BROWDER FILE:
22 Essays on the African American Experience

by Anthony T. Browder
$20.00

Published 1989

"In his 22 Essays on the African American Experience, Tony Browder motivates us to establish the re-birth of our consciousness as a personal goal and a group goal. Experience *From The Browder File*, and incorporate Brother Browder's thought provoking information into your plan for moving from *disintegration* to *reintegration* for our people."
From the Introduction by Dr. Asa G. Hilliard, III

"Essays in this book are not intellectual pontifications. The thought provoking material represents a true labor of love from an African American father, "brother," scholar and "Hue-Man" being who is unlocking the last remaining vestiges of enslavement....."
Patricia A. Newton MD, Psychiatrist

"Each messenger is a specialist. Imhotep shared *medicine*, Hatshepsut shared *liberation*, Jesus shared *love*, Muhammed shared *truth*, Frederick Douglass shared *equality*, Marcus Garvey shared *economics*, Martin Luther King shared *justice*, Dick Gregory shares *health* and Tony Browder shares *knowledge*."
Cathy Hughes, Owner/General Manager WOL-AM/WMMJ-FM, Washington, DC

Exploding the Myths Vol. 1:
NILE VALLEY
CONTRIBUTIONS TO
CIVILIZATION

by Anthony T. Browder
$25.00

Published 1992

Exploding The Myths Vol. I: Nile Valley Contributions To Civilization is an in-depth examination of Nile Valley (Egyptian) civilization and its influence in the development of contemporary culture. This 288 page text is beautifully illustrated with 200 photographs, 150 illustrations, 10 maps, 7 charts and a glossary.

"Tony Browder is one of the latest of a number of messengers attempting to tell the story of the Nile Valley contribution to civilization. In his book, *Nile Valley Contributions to Civilization*, Tony Browder has associated himself with some top-level academic company. He is both a teacher and a learner. In both cases he has done well."

From the Introduction by Dr. John Henrik Clarke

*MY FRIST TRIP
TO AFRICA*

by Atlantis Tye Browder
w/ Anthony T. Browder
$8.95

Published 1991

My First Trip To Africa chronicles the experience of 7-year-old Atlantis during a 13-day study tour to Egypt with her father, her grandmother and 31 other people in November, 1989.

My First Trip To Africa provides young folks and adults with a deeper understanding of ancient Egypt and its relationship to modern America, as seen through the eyes of a child. The narrative was written specifically for children and will assist them in understanding aspects of personal history, world history and African History.

This publication contains 27 photos, 15 illustrations, 3 maps, a glossary and also a parent/teacher guide which includes recommendations for interactive exercises for the child, parent and teacher. This guide is an aid which provides topics of discussion for children in the classroom, at the dinner table or at bedtime.

AFRICA ON MY MIND:
Reflections Of My Second Trip

by Atlantis Tye Browder
w/ Anthony T. Browder
$11.99

Published 1995

Africa On My Mind is the second publication co-authored by Atlantis and her father. It chronicles their experiences while participating in a 15-day study tour to West Africa during the Summer of 1993.

During the course of the study tour Atlantis traveled to Senegal, The Gambia, Ghana and Ivory Coast. She visited numerous cities, villages and historical sites including the infamous slave dungeons at Goree Island, Cape Coast and Elmina.

Written in journal form, the text of *Africa On My Mind* is richly illustrated with 47 photographs, 18 illustrations, 9 maps, 2 charts, a glossary, an index and a list of suggested readings.

The final chapter consists of a conversation between Atlantis and her dad in which they discuss the lingering effects of racism and the historical and cultural significance of their trip.

Annual Study Tours to Egypt
Personally Escorted by Anthony T. Browder

For details contact IKG at 301-853-2465 or online at www.ikg-info.com

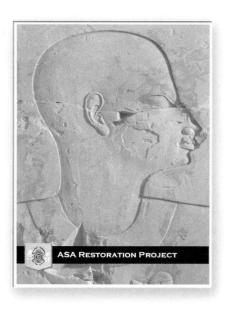

Are you interested in participating in the excavation of a 25th dynasty tomb?

Would you like to help us restore the tomb of Karakhamun in Luxor, Egypt?

For details on how you can contribute to the ASA Restoration Project visit us online at www.asarestorationproject.com

AUDIO AND VIDEO TAPE LIST
By Anthony T. Browder

❑ **#100F** *Nile Valley Contriibutions To Civilization:* The Video: A suitable companion to both Study Guide and Text.
VHS video tape: $40   Time: 80 mins

❑ **#101** *Ancient Egypt: New Perspectives of an African Civilization:* A lecture and slide presentation which features a pictorial and historical overview of ancient Egyptian civilization. Emphasis is placed on the contemporary and historical application of Egyptian philosophy and symbolism.
VHS video tape: $40   Audio tape: $12   Time: 2 hours

❑ **#102** *Egyptian Origins of Science and Metaphysics:* An introduction to ancient knowledge of the human existence within the physical realm (science) and the realm beyond the physical (metaphysical). This lecture features demonstrations on light, color and levitation.
VHS video tape: $40   Audio tape: $12   Time: 2 hours

❑ **#103** *The African Origins of Christianity:* A revealing look at the African influence on religion and the historical and symbolic meaning of the Bible.
VHS video tape: $40   Audic tape: $12   Time: 2 hours

❑ **#104 Spotlight Interviews:** A four part series produced by WHMM-TV at Howard University. An overview of Egyptian History and its impact on civilization; Egyptian Orgins of Science and Metaphysics; an Afrocentric View of Washington, DC.
VHS video tape: $40   Time: 2 hours

❑ **#105** *The Melanin Report:* A review of the "Third Annual Melanin Conference" and a candid discussion of the physical, mental and spiritual aspects of melanin.
Audio tape only: $12   Time: 2 1/2 hrs

Item No.	Quantity	Description	Price Per Item	Total Price

SubTotal: $_____

Shipping & Handling:
($4.00 1st item; $2.00 per each additional item) $_____

TOTAL: $_____

Name_____

Address_____City_____

State_____Zip_____Telephone_____

Make check payable to: THE INSTITUTE OF KARMIC GUIDANCE
PO Box 73025 * Washington, DC 20056 * (301) 853-2465/Fax: (301) 853-7916

To Charge Your Purchase:

Check One: (   ) MASTERCARD   (   ) VISA   (   ) AMERICAN EXPRESS

CARD #_____Exp. Date_____
                                                                              Month / Year

X_____
           Signature required only if charging your purchase

THANK YOU FOR YOUR ORDER
(Please allow 2-3 weeks for delivery)

AUDIO AND VIDEO TAPE LIST
By Anthony T. Browder

❏ **#100F** *Nile Valley Contriibutions To Civilization:* The Video: A suitable companion to both Study Guide and Text.
VHS video tape: $40   Time: 80 mins

❏ **#101** *Ancient Egypt: New Perspectives of an African Civilization:* A lecture and slide presentation which features a pictorial and historical overview of ancient Egyptian civilization. Emphasis is placed on the contemporary and historical application of Egyptian philosophy and symbolism.
VHS video tape: $40   Audio tape: $12   Time: 2 hours

❏ **#102** *Egyptian Origins of Science and Metaphysics:* An introduction to ancient knowledge of the human existence within the physical realm (science) and the realm beyond the physical (metaphysical). This lecture features demonstrations on light, color and levitation.
VHS video tape: $40   Audio tape: $12   Time: 2 hours

❏ **#103** *The African Origins of Christianity:* A revealing look at the African influence on religion and the historical and symbolic meaning of the Bible.
VHS video tape: $40   Audio tape: $12   Time: 2 hours

❏ **#104** **Spotlight Interviews:** A four part series produced by WHMM-TV at Howard University. An overview of Egyptian History and its impact on civilization; Egyptian Orgins of Science and Metaphysics; an Afrocentric View of Washington, DC.
VHS video tape: $40   Time: 2 hours

❏ **#105** *The Melanin Report:* A review of the "Third Annual Melanin Conference" and a candid discussion of the physical, mental and spiritual aspects of melanin.
Audio tape only: $12   Time: 2 1/2 hrs

Item No.	Quantity	Description	Price Per Item	Total Price

SubTotal: $_____

Shipping & Handling:
($4.00 1st item; $2.00 per each additional item) $_____

TOTAL: $_____

Name_____

Address_____City_____

State_____Zip_____Telephone_____

Make check payable to: THE INSTITUTE OF KARMIC GUIDANCE
PO Box 73025 * Washington, DC 20056 * (301) 853-2465/Fax: (301) 853-7916

To Charge Your Purchase:

Check One: ( ) MASTERCARD   ( ) VISA   ( ) AMERICAN EXPRESS

CARD #_____Exp. Date_____
                                                                              Month / Year

X_____
Signature required only if charging your purchase

THANK YOU FOR YOUR ORDER
(Please allow 2-3 weeks for delivery)